Simple C++

Jeffrey M. Cogswell

WAITE GROUP PRESS™

Corte Madera, CA

Publisher: *Mitchell Waite*
Editor-in-Chief: *Scott Calamar*
Editorial Director: *Joel Fugazzotto*
Managing Editor: *John Crudo*
Content Editor: *Harry Henderson*
Technical Reviewer: *Mike Radtke*
Production Director: *Julianne Ososke*
Design: *Cecile Kaufman*
Production: *Cecelia G. Morales*
Illustrations: *David Povalaitis*
Cover Design: *Cecile Kaufman*
Cover Illustration: *David Povalaitis*

Printed in the United States of America
94 95 96 97 • 10 9 8 7 6 5 4 3 2

Cogswell, Jeffrey M., 1968–
    Simple C++ / Jeffrey M. Cogswell.
       p.   cm.
    Includes index.
    ISBN 1-878739-44-1 : $16.95
    1. C++ (Computer program language)   I. Title.
QA76.73.C153C65   1994
005.13'3—dc20

93-44868
CIP

DEDICATION

This book is dedicated to Dr. Gary Chartrand of the Western Michigan University Department of Mathematics and Statistics. Not only did you teach me how to teach, you taught me how to teach through writing . . .

. . . and to Grandpa Anderson, for giving me so many of your great talents, so that I may one day call them my own.

ABOUT THE AUTHOR

Jeff Cogswell has been programming computers since his teenage days with Pet computers and VIC-20s. Since then, he has taught and tutored numerous students in areas including Mathematics and Computer Science. He is presently working as both a Microsoft Windows programmer and a night-time professional writer. He has written for various computer magazines, including *Windows TechJournal* and *Dr. Dobb's Journal*. When he's not writing or programming, he spends his time playing jazz piano and the electric guitar and credits Rachmaninoff and Eddie VanHalen as his influences.

TABLE OF CONTENTS

Part 4: Nuts and Bolts

CONTENTS

Part 2: Dog Talk and Other Useful Languages (Like C++)

Part 4: Nuts and Bolts

ACKNOWLEDGMENTS

I wish I could put this section in a place where everyone would read it. It's tempting to put a little warning at the beginning of Chapter 1, saying, "Hey, you'd better read the Acknowledgments, or you won't understand the first 50 pages." But that wouldn't be true, and it would be a bit rude, anyway. So to those who are reading this right now, I thank you!

It's amazing how many people it takes to write a book. So many people helped out that there wasn't room to list all their names on the front cover. I'm not even sure why my name is there—many of these people worked as hard as I did.

Unfortunately, being an absent-minded programmer and an absent-minded writer (which, contrary to popular belief, amounts to absent-minded squared, not simply absent-minded times two), I am bound to forget some people. If you are one of these missed people, I apologize; don't take it personally, it's just me. I promise to give you extra space in my next book. (Remind me!)

First, thanks to everyone at The Waite Group, including:

- Mitch Waite, for conceiving this book, and giving me the chance to write it, and for injecting your wonderful creativity into it.

- The editors—Scott Calamar, John Crudo, Harry Henderson, and Mike Radtke—for working so hard, as if the book were your own. I'd like to point out that a few sentences here and there were actually written by Harry, who managed to mimic my style perfectly. Whoever would guess that the reference to a fictional Mrs. Gribbles was Harry's writing, not mine? Not to mention occasional references to pizzas!

- And, of course, to everyone else at TWG. You people have been great to work with, and I can't wait to write my next book for Waite Group Press!

Thanks to my "beta-readers" for reading some of the early text in its rough states and providing fantastic suggestions for improving the book. Here they are, in no particular order: Kelly O'Connor, Heather Russell, Jim Herman, Carol Carver, Lisa Landis, Brad Murphy, and last but certainly not least, Kristy Huang. Extra special thanks to Joan Karen Sides for all the creative inspiration, and for laughing hardest at my humor.

Special thanks to the folks who gave me a chance and believed in me, and helped to shape and mold me: Jeff Miller, Linda Close, J. D. Hildebrand, Ron Burk, Andrew Schulman, and Tom Swan.

Thanks to those who have most greatly influenced my writing. I hope to meet all of you some day. You are: Orson Scott Card (author of lots and lots of science fiction/fantasy novels), Douglas Adams (author of *The Hitchhiker's Guide to the Galaxy*), Gary Larsen (author and artist of *The Far Side* comic), the guys in Pink Floyd, famous musician Peter Gabriel, and, of course, all the guys in *Monty Python's Flying Circus*.

Very, very special thanks to the people who taught me how to teach: Dr. Gary Chartrand, Dr. Ghidewon Abay "Gidean" Asmerom, Ms. Barbara Smith, and Mr. Bill Talsma. You have not only shown me how to Tell and Explain, but to Show and Teach.

Thanks to Mom, Dad, and Grandpa Anderson (Pat Cogswell, Dave Cogswell, and Elmer Anderson) for giving me my talents. I miss you, Grandpa, and I hope you read this book from up there in heaven.

Thanks, of course, to all the wonderful folks at Q+E Software, Inc., especially the Multilink/VB team for understanding when I just couldn't keep up with your 60-hour-week schedules. (Of course, now that the book's done, I have no excuses!) Thanks especially to Ed Glass, Julia Trimmer, Rowland Archer, and Justin Pinnix.

And an extra-special thanks again to Kristy Huang for just being there and cheering me on.

Dear Reader:

What is a book? Is it perpetually fated to be inky words on a paper page? Or can a book simply be something that inspires—feeding your head with ideas and creativity regardless of the medium? The latter, I believe. That's why I'm always pushing our books to a higher plane; using new technology to reinvent the medium.

I wrote my first book in 1973, *Projects in Sights, Sounds, and Sensations.* I like to think of it as our first multimedia book. In the years since then, I've learned that people want to experience information, not just passively absorb it—they want interactive MTV in a book. With this in mind, I started my own publishing company and published *Master C,* a book/disk package that turned the PC into a C language instructor. Then we branched out to computer graphics with *Fractal Creations,* which included a color poster, 3-D glasses, and a totally rad fractal generator. Ever since, we've included disks and other goodies with most of our books. *Virtual Reality Creations* is bundled with 3-D Fresnel viewing goggles and *Walkthroughs and Flybys CD* comes with a multimedia CD-ROM. We've made complex multimedia accessible for any PC user with *Ray Tracing Creations, Multimedia Creations, Making Movies on Your PC, Image Lab,* and three books on Fractals.

The Waite Group continues to publish innovative multimedia books on cutting-edge topics, and of course the programming books that make up our heritage. Being a programmer myself, I appreciate clear guidance through a tricky OS, so our books come bundled with disks and CDs loaded with code, utilities and custom controls.

By 1994, The Waite Group will have published 135 books. Our next step is to develop a new type of book, an interactive, multimedia experience involving the reader on many levels. With this new book, you'll be trained by a computer-based instructor with infinite patience, run a simulation to visualize the topic, play a game that shows you different aspects of the subject, interact with others on-line, and have instant access to a large database on the subject. For traditionalists, there will be a full-color, paper-based book.

In the meantime, they've wired the White House for hi-tech; the information super highway has been proposed; and computers, communication, entertainment, and information are becoming inseparable. To travel in this Digital Age you'll need guidebooks. The Waite Group offers such guidance for the most important software—your mind.

We hope you enjoy this book. For a color catalog, just fill out and send in the Reader Report Card at the back of the book.

Mitchell Waite

Mitchell Waite
Publisher

INTRODUCTION: ANYONE CAN LEARN C++! REALLY!

This book is not like other computer books. Although many authors make such a claim, one quick scan through Chapter 1 should prove that point. In this book you will witness a science-fiction story providing clues into the facts about C++ and object-oriented programming. And even though it's science fiction, the programming topics explained are for real.

So what do you need to know before you read this book?

How to read.

Really! That's about all you need.

Well, okay, you also might want to have a computer handy, but honestly, even that's not a prerequisite. Indeed, there are sample programs in this book, but you can even skip those and still manage to pick up an awful lot about C++ and object-oriented programming.

So what exactly does that mean? It means you can learn C++ as a first computer language! That concept is entirely new to the programming world, and most people who already know a lot about programming would probably scoff at such an idea. But I have a feeling that you, the reader, will disprove the notion that C++ can't be learned as a first language.

Indeed, most computer books teaching C++ assume you already know C. And those that don't assume that are nearly impossible to read, so you might as well know C first.

By the way, a quick tip on reading this book. If you've read other computer books, you've no doubt run into the situation where you read a confusing paragraph and have to reread it several times until you finally understand it. Why do you do that? Because you know that if you don't get it now, you probably won't understand the next topic.

As much as writers like to avoid this situation by making all paragraphs easy to read, sometimes it just doesn't work. Not all people learn the same way, and an explanation that works for one person may not work for you. So I've tried to recognize those situations and follow the confusing paragraph with another paragraph that re-explains the topic in another manner.

It boils down to this: If you read a paragraph and don't follow it completely, *don't worry about it!* Just go on to the next one. Besides, really, nothing's *that* important. If you find you still don't understand it and realize later that you need it, go back and try again. But don't sweat it. You'll pick it up sooner or later.

Also, if for some reason you don't really want to learn how to actually write programs, but just want to understand more *about* programming, then this book is prefect for you. That's because you can safely skip the sample programs at the end of each chapter, as well as the entire program samples section (Part 3), and still learn gobs and gobs of information. "Gobs and gobs," of course, is simliar to "billions and billions," but far less specific.

Before You Begin

Unfortunately, there are a couple things you need to do before you can begin. (If you plan on doing the sample programs, that is.) First, you need to install your compiler, if it's not already on your computer. I wish I could list every compiler and every computer here and give quick instructions on how to do it, but alas, that simply isn't possible. However, the installation is usually pretty easy, and the manuals always explain how. If you're using a UNIX system or a large computer such as a VAX, the compiler is probably already installed.

If you do need to install the compiler, you may be asked a fairly simple question, such as "Do you want to install the samples?" or a rather cryptic computer-sounding question like, "Which memory models do you want to install?" Your easiest bet is to accept the defaults (if there are any), and make sure to answer yes for the samples.

After the compiler is installed, you need to know how to type in a program and compile it. There's probably a quick sample in the manual that you might want to go through. Don't bother trying to learn about programming from that sample; that's what this book is for. The main goal is to learn how to type in programs and save them to disk, and how to compile and link them. (We'll look at those two words shortly.)

On some computers, such as Macs or PCs running Windows, you can double-click on the compiler icon, and that'll bring you into the right place to type in the program. You can usually save your programs by choosing a File menu and Save, or something similar to that. The manual will tell you for sure.

On other computers, you may have to type in the name of an editor, such as VI or EMACS or B or EDIT or ED. The VI editor is pretty complicated, and you'll probably require the help of a manual or some kind person. Check the manual for details on how to save the files.

After you have typed in and saved your programs, you'll need to know how to compile and link them. *Compiling* is the process where the computer converts your program files into a form your computer can understand and the *compiler* performs this conversion. *Linking* is where it connects your program to some of its internal systems.

On some Macs and Windows computers, you can often just choose Compile or Build or Run from a menu. Other computers will have a command to type at the prompt, such as perhaps CC to compile and LINK to link. Check the manual for details.

Sometime you'll be compiling programs consisting of several files, called modules. You'll need to know how to do that; on some Macs and Windows computers you can create what's called a Project and add all your files to this project. On other computers you'll use what's known as a Make file. The compiler probably has a sample you can use as a guide, and you'll definitely want to take a look at the manual for help here.

Finally, after your program is compiled and linked, you need to know how to run it. On some Macs and Windows computers, you do this by choosing the Run menu. On other computers, you simply type the name of your program to run it.

Part 1
Robodog

1

BUILDING THE INCREDIBLE ROBOT DOG

"Bark, bark, ruff, ruff."
(Translation: Computers are animals, too.)

It's the mid-1990s and we work for a state-of-the-art robotics company called PEts That Think, or PETT. PEts That Think was founded for the purpose of providing consumers with the most advanced robotics available. Their latest and greatest product is the Incredible Robot Dog, or IRD. The IRD is the newest breed of dog, made of only the finest stainless steel components. No dent in its side is too big for a small sledgehammer to repair. Should it break down, any other IRD that happens to be in the vicinity can fix it in a flash. And when you order one, the IRD comes complete with a fine set of oriental knives that can handle any job it can't.

The Incredible Robot Dogs are capable of many things, but their main purposes in life are to serve as communication devices, watchdogs, and advanced dustbusters.

Our job here at PETT involves working as part of a team developing what are called programs for the IRD. A program is simply a set of instructions that tells a computer what to do. While the rest of our team is working on the watchdog program, which instructs the IRD how to respond to intruders, we have a different assignment. Our job is to write a program that tells an IRD how to perform its daily routine of eating, sleeping, playing, and so forth.

We came to work as a junior programmer at PETT because they're one of the best high tech consumer electronics and robotics companies around, and they have good benefits, too. Our department doesn't yet use the hot new language C++, but we plan to learn it and move up in the company.

PETT's engineering department has already adopted C++, because it is a powerful yet easy-to-learn language. In fact, many companies these days are using it. For now, though, we'd better get to work on the IRD's daily routines.

Before we dive into the programming itself, let's carefully think the process through. The boss prefers we do it that way, anyway. First, let's state the entire procedure in plain, concise English.

We want to create the IRD's daily routine. It should do the following, in this order:

- Wake up.
- Eat leftover pizza.
- Go potty.
- Eat biscuits.

- 🦴 Walk.
- 🦴 Eat puppy chow.
- 🦴 Play.
- 🦴 Eat snack.
- 🦴 Go potty.
- 🦴 Sleep.

That's pretty good for our purposes. But to get it into the computer, we have to make sure it's in a special format and only uses words provided us by the folks down in engineering who built this version of the IRD. To find out what the proper format is, we need to look it up in the *IRD Programmer's Manual.*

The *IRD Programmer's Manual* is like all computer manuals: In addition to a Ph.D., it requires the reader to have a complete knowledge of the book's topic. There are no examples—the authors felt their explanations were so thorough, there was no need for examples. Also, this particular version of the manual is the high-tech kind, with its own little keyboard and computer monitor and headphones. We're pretty sure it was made into computer form to hide the fact that in paper form it would be over 7,500 pages, stretch across 11 volumes, and weigh more than 40 pounds. Typical computer book.

After a long struggle with the *IRD Programmer's Manual* , we eventually reach the section on the proper format for programming the IRD. Here is the correct format for our program:

```
daily
{
  wake;
  eat (pizza);
  potty;
  eat (biscuits);
  walk;
  eat (puppychow);
  play;
  eat (snack);
  potty;
  sleep;
}
```

This means, "The procedure for the 'daily' routine consists of the steps: wake, eat pizza, potty, eat biscuits, walk, eat puppychow, play, eat snack, potty, sleep." The curly brackets—{ and }—tell the computer where the steps begin and end. Each step ends with a semicolon.

Besides learning the correct formatting procedure, we have also run into two new words: command and parameter. *Command* in this context means about the same as it does when programming our real dog at home. It's a word that tells the dog to do something, such as eat, walk, and play.

Parameter refers to the words that occasionally follow the commands, such as (pizza), (biscuits), and (snacks). Parameters are usually nouns.

For example, in

```
eat (pizza)
```

eat is a command and (pizza) is a parameter. It seems that commands are verbs, and parameters are objects—just like in Ms. Gribble's English class. Please note that the parameter is always (inside parentheses).

If we forget what a parameter is, we can look it up (or any of the new words we'll be learning) in the glossary.

For all its flaws, the *IRD Programmer's Manual* is all we've got, so we'll continue to refer to it occasionally. Now, however, it's time to get our goobledygook straight from the nerd's mouth—in other words, it's time to visit engineering. (It's in the basement, of course.)

Oops

As soon as we arrive in the engineering department, we visit the head engineer, Bill, and ask him what's happening. We see he's working at a computer screen, designing the abilities of the next revision of the IRD, which they imaginatively call IRD TWO. Bill is hard at work, filling in the details of a list that appears on his computer screen. Figure 1-1 shows a sample of his screen.

Looking at the screen, we notice that all the headings mention a part of the dog, such as eyes or mouth. Bill calls these *objects* of the dog. The words beneath the objects are the abilities each object has, such as "to eat."

Chatting with Bill, we find he not only gives the objects abilities (which he insists on calling *methods*), but he also gives them lists of things and values. For instance, he specifies that the Mouth object is to have a list of foods it likes, and a list of foods it can't stand. Bill doesn't actually fill in these values and lists right now; he simply states that

Figure 1-1 Bill's computer screen

they're there. This is because each IRD is different and will have its own likes and dislikes. Bill calls these values and lists *attributes,* since these things give certain attributes to the different objects. Figure 1-2 shows some of the IRD's objects and attributes, and Figure 1-3 shows the objects listed with their abilities (or methods) and attributes.

Notice in Figure 1-2 that the eye has for one attribute a "list of objects the eye recognizes." Again, since each actual dog is different, the list will be different for each dog, and will be filled in when the programmers customize each dog to the customer's taste.

After we return from looking at Figure 1-3, we find that Bill's still droning on about programming. It seems he didn't even notice we'd left. But he does say something that catches our attention: "I'm assigning abilities—or methods—and attributes for each object in the dog. The legs, the eyes, the mouth, the ears, are all objects, and I'm giving each their own sets of attributes and methods. Since I'm concentrating individually on each object in the dog, I call it object-oriented programming." We notice that on the screen the words object-oriented programming are abbreviated OOP. Under our breath, we say, "That's pretty profound." Bill doesn't notice the sarcasm in our voice, and he says, "Profound! Fantastic! Profound Object-Oriented Programming! The POOP method!"

Figure 1-2 The IRD's Eye and Mouth objects with their attributes

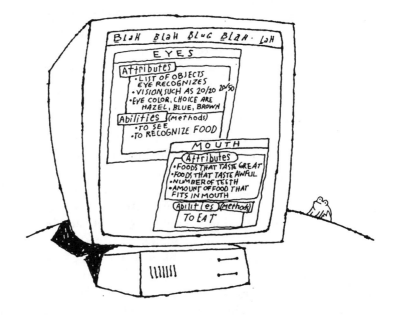

Figure 1-3 The IRD's Eye and Mouth objects with both attributes
and methods

So, apparently, object-oriented programming concentrates on taking a thing, (like the Incredible Robot Dog), and breaking it down into objects (like the eyes, the ears, the legs) and assigning methods and attributes (like lists of food) to each object. Hmmm. So that's what that's all about!

The Main Event

We bid bye bye to Boring Bill and move on to the office of his co-worker, Linda Pavlov. Linda is part of the IRD development team too, and like Bill, she's working at a computer. Her screen looks a lot more interesting than Bill's did, however. Though half of it is another list of words, the other half is a picture of an IRD. And something fascinating is happening: as Dr. Pavlov pulls a dog biscuit out of her desk, the IRD on the screen begins to drool!

Linda then touches the screen where the dog is, and he barks. It's as if he could feel it. She explains that she's taking the abilities (or methods) and attributes put together by Bill and attaching outside-world events to them. For every outside-world event, she assigns a set of things that are to happen in order: certain attributes change, and specified abilities (or methods) take place. For instance, when she places food in front of the dog, the eyes' food-recognition ability does its thing. Then the Saliva-Level attribute increases to 100 percent, which means the IRD drools. Take a look at Figure 1-4 for a list of some of Linda's work.

Linda explains that what we have just seen—drooling at the sight of food—is an example of what is called *event-driven programming*. Something happens in the real world (the biscuit), which triggers a particular piece of program (the drool). This is cause-and-effect programming; the event "drives" the response.

She tells us we may have seen event-driven programming before. We have seen event-driven programming in software packages, such as any program on the Macintosh or on an IBM-compatible PC running Microsoft Windows. Or, she points out, we may have seen it at the bridal registry department at a local store, or in a state welcome center on a large highway. We remember seeing a computer screen that showed a map of the entire state with county lines drawn in, and when we touched a county a zoomed-in picture of the county appeared (see Figure 1-5).

Linda says, "The people who built those machines with their touch-screens used event-driven programming. They had to tell the computer

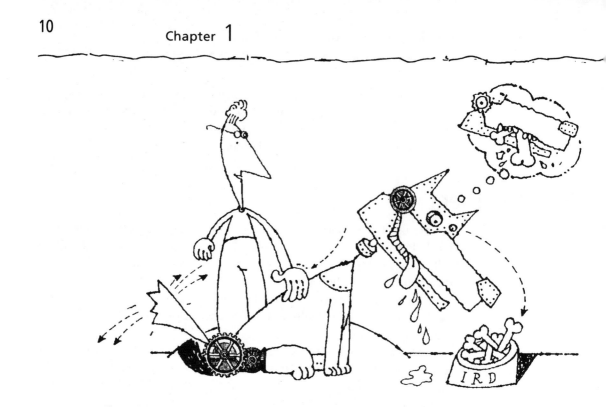

Figure 1-4 External events and the methods that occur and attributes that change

Figure 1-5 A touch-screen and a map, often found at tourist centers

how to respond when the touch-screen is touched in different places. Like most programming, they had to be very specific, right down to tracking the exact position of the finger on the screen. A slight shift to the right, for instance, might put the finger on a different county, and so that different county must be drawn instead."

Remember, the reason it's called event-driven programming is that the resulting program responds to various real-world events. Also remember that when writing an event-driven style program, we use the methods and attributes set forth in the object-oriented aspect of programming.

And in object-oriented programming, we concentrate on the individual objects. In the case of the IRD, these objects were just words on the screen representing the objects comprising the IRD: the legs, the eyes, the mouth, and so on, along with their methods and attributes. Legs have the ability to run, and speed can differ for each IRD. Eyes have the ability to recognize things, and can recognize different kinds of food.

It's important to note that what you saw on the screen were simply words and numbers *representing* these methods and attributes. Generally, that's the case. For instance, the computer version of our checkbook, just like our actual check register, only represents the actual money moving in and (more often) out of our wallet. It isn't really the money; it only represents or simulates it.

The Good Old Days

After leaving Linda Pavlov's office, we go to make our final visit for the day. This time it's with old Dr. Samuel William Smith. Rumor has it he's over 90 years old and still working just as well as he was 50 years ago. The staff here at PETT affectionately calls him Dr. Old.

We enter Dr. Old's office and find him sitting in a yoga position on a small mat on the floor.

"Well, well!" he shouts as he leaps to his feet. "Ready to learn about the good old days of programming?"

We look at him questioningly.

"Sure! The good old days, long before this newfangled object-oriented stuff."

We explain that we're really not supposed to be learning about other types of programming. Our job is to learn about object-oriented programming.

"I understand completely," he says, "but there are some things you need to learn first. For instance, each of an object's methods performs a task. This could be any number of things. But a method may also give us back something. For instance, the mouth may have a method that lets other objects find out which foods the mouth likes and doesn't like, and the eyes may need this information. So how do the eyes actually get the information? Simple. The eye's recognition method activates— calls—the mouth's method for listing the foods the IRD likes. This method then sends a list back to the eyes. That is, it returns a list. And that list is the foods the IRD likes. Get it?"

We think about that. The recognition activates or calls the mouth's List-Food method, which gives back a list of foods the IRD likes. Simple enough. We tell him we understand.

"Good!" he says. "Now understand this: Not all methods give back something. Some just do something and go on their merry way and don't give us back any information. We just trust that the programmers who

wrote the method knew what they were doing, and that the method did it right.

"Oh," he continues. "One more thing. These methods each perform a specific function. So we can also call them *functions*. Other things qualify as functions too, but methods are one particular case of functions. Don't get too hung up on that just yet. You've learned a lot today. Just remember that we discussed it, and feel free to come back to me later if you need me to repeat any of it or go into further detail."

We thank him and leave his office.

Don't Panic

If you picked up a few things along the way, don't panic. Your brain won't get over-saturated with some of the stuff here. (And if does, feel free to get rid of some of it. You can always look it up later.) But, briefly, here's some stuff we looked at:

- commands
- parameters
- objects
- methods
- attributes
- object-oriented programming
- event-driven programming
- functions

The glossary in the back of the book lists the definitions of these words if you want to review. But you can wait until tomorrow to do that.

Go Get Yourself a Pizza

Well, that's enough reading for one day. Feel free to take a break before you read the next section, which is optional anyway. After all, we don't want to cram too much of this stuff in our brains. We need the space for more important things, like remembering the phone number of the nearest pizza joint.

Chapter 1

Program Section

Most of the chapters in this book end with a Program Section. If you prefer to learn *about* programming, and not how to actually program, then you can safely skip these without risk of falling behind. But if you wish to learn about how you can work with C++, then the Program Sections are for you.

Although we will be referring to the imaginary IRD, the programs and techniques here are for real. We will be using C++ to write programs that could control an IRD, if one really existed.

Program Flow

Computers do things step by step, just as our imaginary program tells the IRD how to do things step by step for a daily routine. Even in the case of event-driven programming, where pieces of our program (or *code*) get activated in response to real-world events, the computer must perform a sequence of activities one step at a time: When the event occurs and the corresponding piece of our program gets activated, the computer begins to step through the piece of code.

The computer can jump to another piece of code, but it still does it in sequence over time. It never does two things at once. (Some computers can do what's known as multitasking—that is, perform several things at once. But for the C++ programming we'll be doing, we won't concern ourselves with multitasking.)

Just as we did in our imaginary program, when we're programming in C++, we specify program statements by typing in lines of code on the screen. We end each statement with a semicolon (;). Statements can actually be broken up into more than one line, in which case the last line of the entire statement must normally end with a semicolon. If you want, you might take a quick scan at some of the programs at the end of Chapter 2. Don't worry if they don't make sense to you; mainly notice how most lines end in a semicolon.

Format

Computers are picky about *format* of the programs—what the programs look like—at least to a point. Take a glance again at some of the programs in Chapter 2, and notice how the words are separated by spaces. In C++ we must make sure we separate words with a space or a tab or a carriage return. There are exceptions, and we'll look at these exceptions when we need them. The first exception is that we don't need a space between a line's final word and the semicolon.

We are free to have as many spaces as we want between words, and we can even mix spaces, tabs, and carriage returns. We can also indent lines as far as we want, and have several blank lines separating lines of code. The idea, however, is not to see how creative we can be in drawing a pretty picture out of the program, but rather to separate lines of code so that they make sense, providing some sort of visual cue for humans who have to look at the program and figure out what's going on. (The computer ignores indentations, extra spaces, and blank lines when it runs the program.)

Variables, Math, and All That

Computers can remember things quite well. Not only do they remember things, they remember *specific* things. For example, our IRD doesn't just remember what an IRDApple is, he remembers the IRDApple he ate yesterday that was rotten in the middle; and the one last week that was so good but made the IRD's stomach upset (it figures!).

On the other hand, for each specific thing the computer remembers, it must know what kind of thing it is. For instance, the IRD must remember not just the food it ate yesterday that was rotten in the middle, but what kind of food it was: an IRDApple. The IRD must also remember amounts: the amount of energy left; the amount of food needed to restore the energy; the distance to the nearest fire hydrant. And, as before, it must know what kind of amount: that is, if it's a whole number (called *integer*, represented in C++ by the word *int*) or a decimal number (called *floating-point*, represented in C++ by the word *float*).

One way to look at the way computers remember things is to imagine the computer as having a sheet of notebook paper filled with horizontal lines. When we start a new program, the computer provides us (figuratively speaking) with such a sheet of paper, and each line on the paper is used to remember a separate thing. It would look something like Figure 1-6.

The first column has the type of thing: integer, floating-point number, IRDApple, or whatever.

In order for us to keep things straight (since we could have two different lines both holding integers), we must give each line a unique name.

type	name
int	height
int	weight
float	energysupply
IRDApple	ThisApple

Figure 1-6 Computer memory as a sheet of notebook paper

For instance, suppose we want a program to have two integers, a floating-point number, and an IRDApple. This name goes in the last column.

When we type in the program, we'd be typing it in like this:

```
int         height;
int         weight;
float       energysupply;
IRDApple    ThisApple;
```

Later, but not necessarily immediately, we would give values to each one. For instance, we might provide the following:

type	name	value
int	height	10
int	weight	20
IRDApple	ThisApple	RED

We call each of these lines *variables* and the names *variable names*. The kinds of variables are called *types*. Don't try to memorize these words now. You'll pick them up soon enough, because they're used almost all the time in computer programming.

2
PUT THE DOG OUT TO PLAY

Today we'll start with a visit to Bill to get some answers to a few questions we've been wondering about.

"Bill," we begin, but before we can say any more, Bill is pounding our back in an apparent welcoming ritual while simultaneously exclaiming how *wonderful* it is to see us again. Evidently the robot dog isn't the only thing around here that needs some more social skills.

"Bill," we continue, "before we go any further in this book, you've got to tell us how to pronounce this."

A Weird Name for a Programming Language?

"See-plus-plus," he replies at once. We ask where the language came from.

"Why do you want to know? Programmers aren't supposed to care about stuff like that."

"Well, we're not your typical programmer. We're a lot more normal than your typical programmer."

"Ok, ok. C++ is the next step up the evolutionary ladder from the C language. The C language was developed by Dennis Ritchie of Bell Laboratories in the early 1970s. As bigger and more powerful computers appeared, they naturally required more complex programs. The earlier languages—FORTRAN, for example, or BASIC—would get so tangled up in themselves that they became virtually impossible to understand.

And because of this, programs written in these earlier languages could be very difficult to fix. C took a new approach, called structured programming, that permitted the new larger programs to be broken up into smaller modular components. The results were so successful that C became the dominant programming language of the 1980s.

"As for the '++' part of the name C++," he adds, "it's called that because, as I just told you, in C the symbols ++ mean to add one. And the inventors of C++ basically added to the current language, C. Actually, they added more than one. Later, in another chapter, we'll explore some of the differences."

Goodness, he's living life as a computer textbook. . . . But we agree; let's wait until later to talk about that. It's getting a little too deep for now.

Bill asks what the other thing was that we wanted to talk about.

We start out calmly telling him we were reading about these things called parameters in the *IRD Programmer's Manual*. But as we recall how it was completely impossible to read, we feel our blood pressure rising and we're soon yelling. Bill steps back a bit and waits for us to calm down. He then decides to take a go at explaining them.

"They're really quite simple," he begins.

We remind him that if they were so darn simple, we wouldn't be asking for an explanation. "Hmm, maybe Bill wrote the *IRD Programmer's Manual*," we wonder quietly.

Since he values our friendship (and wants to borrow five bucks for lunch) he apologizes and starts to oh-so-briefly explain the missing part.

Oh-So-Briefly

Bill says that when you are programming, you have to set up the methods, as he explained yesterday.

"For instance, suppose you want to teach the dog how to eat. You must first consider the object that does the eating, which is the mouth. You then give it a method: eating. But you're not done yet. You must tell the dog *how* to implement this method."

"Implement?" we ask. "You mean 'how to *do* this method?'"

"Uh, yeah."

Typical programmer, we think to ourselves. Always gotta substitute a three-syllable word when a one-syllable word will do. Bill continues, "Anyway, you have to tell the computer how to implement the method.

So just how do you tell the dog how to eat?" We realize this isn't gonna be so brief after all, and settle down for a whole new section.

The Wonders of Healthy Digestion

"Basically," Bill continues, "we can't just tell the dog to eat. We have to tell it *how* to eat. For instance, we might describe the process of eating with the following steps." He approaches the chalkboard and writes:

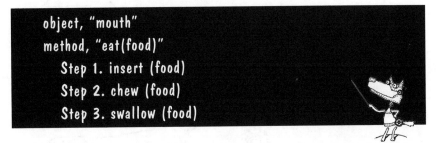

```
object, "mouth"
method, "eat(food)"
    Step 1. insert (food)
    Step 2. chew (food)
    Step 3. swallow (food)
```

He reminds us that the parameters are the words in parentheses.

He rambles on some more. "All this means that when the IRD needs to eat, his brain pulls up its little computerized file folder, and first looks up the object he's dealing with—in this case, 'mouth.' He then looks up the method he needs—in this case, 'eat.' He sees that to eat he needs a food (the parameter). He makes sure he has a food (whatever that is) and then uses it in the step-by-step instructions: insert it, chew it, and swallow it."

We think about that, and something dawns on us: How does the IRD know how to insert something, chew it, and swallow it? We ask Bill.

Bill, being an all-knowing computer programmer (just ask him), continues. "This is how: Those abilities are themselves methods for other objects. The dog's lips and tongue together make the object that inserts the food. The dog's teeth comprise the object that chews the food, and the throat is the object that swallows food. And somewhere else in our program we have to have a section explaining how to do *those*."

"Remember," he says, "we have to divide the IRD into objects, and those objects have methods and attributes. The mouth, the lips, the throat, the teeth, are all objects, and each has methods. And it's interesting that when we describe these methods, we use other methods. For instance, we used the Insert, Chew, and Swallow methods to describe the Eat method."

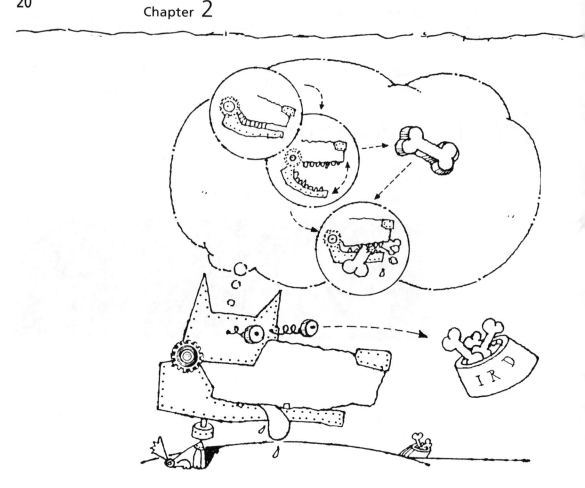

Hold on! Where does this circular logic end? You can't describe one method with other methods forever. Eventually, you must run out of methods.

"Good point! Somewhere, we need basic objects and methods that the computer already knows how to do. And those objects include numbers, with methods like adding, subtracting, and so on. Everything can be broken down eventually into those basic objects and methods, believe it or not. When we start building some of our own objects in C++, we'll see how that works."

Which Came First, the Program or the Object?

One more question for Bill: When we write a new program, and the computer executes it, where does the computer start?

Bill says, "There will be a section of the program called *main*. This is where it begins."

That's good enough for now. We'll think about that some more later. We leave Bill and head back to our office upstairs.

Meanwhile, Back at the Office

After stopping at the snack machine and trying to forget about all this programming stuff for a while, we arrive back at our office. There's a voice-mail message from Bill:

> Hi, it's me. You left your wallet down here. When you pick it up, don't worry. Nobody stole five bucks. I just borrowed it for my lunch, that's all. Also, if you're doing any C++ programming, I thought I'd mention one more thing: the *main* is actually a method for the entire program. Think about that. Hey, cool, a credit card's in your wallet, too. In that case, I'll be back in two weeks with a dark tan. Have a nice couple of weeks without me! I'll forward my phone to yours. See ya!

Well, next time we need help, we'll just ask Linda Pavlov. She seems a little friendlier, anyway. But the joke will be on Bill: We'll let him put the plane ticket on the credit card and *then* we'll report the card stolen, after he's already stuck in who-knows-where.

Now, what was that he said about main? It's a method for the entire program. Hmmm. The main, he said earlier, is where the program starts. Hey, that makes sense! The program itself is an object, and the main is the Main method! It describes *how* to do the program! And the computer has no choice but to start with the main!

We'll have to review some of this tomorrow, because we can only learn so much in one day. The excess gets shoved into that really cool part of the brain known as short-term memory (that's the part that helped us ace our history tests in school).

Don't Panic

Okay, let's see what happened today.

We finally found out where the name C++ comes from and that it's pronounced "see-plus-plus."

We also figured out that we need to tell the computer how to do each method, and that somewhere buried deep in the machine is a set of basic methods it already knows about. When telling the computer how to do the methods, we use other methods and the basic methods.

We then realized that we call the part of the program that starts things the main part of the program.

But enough about that stuff. We'd rather free up our brain for other things. Like watching TV.

Stuck Without Plastic Money

Now put the book down, turn on the TV, and forget about C++ for a while. Don't worry, it won't go away (whether that's good or bad, well, who knows?). Then later, if you want, you can explore the following Program Section. Besides, the news should be coming on soon, and maybe there will be a story about an American stuck in jail in some faraway place for trying to use a stolen credit card.

Program Section

Finally, a First C++ Program

Before you can type in a C++ program, you have to know a little bit about your computer. (Not much, I promise.) You need to know how to enter stuff into an editor, save it, and compile it (see the Introduction for some notes about this).

After you figure out how to save files with the editor, type in the following program, Listing 2-1. Like the fake program we looked at in the first chapter, it doesn't matter how far you indent things. It also doesn't matter if you put extra blank lines in between lines of code. But it *does* matter that you get the uppercase and lowercase right.

Listing 2-1 First HELLO.CPP

```
#include <iostream.h>
void main()
{
  cout << "Hello, Mr. IRD!";
}
```

As with the fake program we looked at earlier, lines inside the curly brackets {} must end with a semicolon. (That's not really the complete rule about curly brackets {}, but for now we're safe to follow it. We'll look at the full rule later, when we need it.) Also, spaces must separate distinct words, and there can be as many spaces as you want.

Type in the program and save it as HELLO.CPP. Compile and run it, and watch the people around you look on in amazement as they see the following appear on:

> **Hello, Mr. IRD!**

If you get some errors, check to make sure that you typed in the code exactly as it appears here. If you typed in something wrong, go ahead and make the changes and congratulate yourself, because you've just seen something you'll see every day in the world of programming: error messages. They're a fact of life. Remember, don't take it personally. Even the famous programmers see error messages daily. (Well, the rich ones do, anyway; there's no such thing as a famous programmer.)

You might also get some messages called *warnings*. Often you can ignore these. If you do get some, read them. If they make sense, great; if not, don't worry too much. Just make sure the program is typed in exactly as shown, and don't worry about the warnings yet.

Let's quickly skim through the small program above, looking at things in order of importance rather than in order of appearance.

First, let's look at the words *void main*. These introduce the Main method, which tells the computer what to do first. (The word *void* means the method doesn't return anything to the computer after it's finished. Remember Dr. Old's talk about methods returning things? In the next chapter, we'll see an example of a Main method returning something to the computer.)

The computer starts the program by executing what immediately follows the first brace, {, and finishes when it finishes the last line prior to main's closing brace, }. In this case, that means executing the one line,

```
cout << "Hello, Mr. IRD!";
```

This line tells the computer to print on the screen the words Hello, Mr. IRD! It works like this: The double less-than symbols, <<, instruct the computer to send what follows to what comes first. In this case, send the words Hello, Mr. IRD! to the Cout ("see-out") object, which generally represents the screen.

Now back to cout. We could have several cout lines and even pile some stuff onto one line, as shown in Listing 2-2.

Listing 2-2 Second HELLO.CPP

```
#include <iostream.h>
void main()
{
  cout << "Hello, Mr. IRD!" << endl << "It's good";
  cout << " to see you again. So how";
  cout << " are the kids?";
}
```

This program prints the following on the screen:

Hello, Mr. IRD!

It's good to see you again. So how are the kids?

Notice there's some extra stuff in the first cout line in the program, and the words "It's good" showed up on the second line in the output. (*Output* is the computer term for the stuff that showed up on the screen.)

This happened because the word *endl* (for "end line") told the computer to end the current line and move to the next line of output. Every time we want to give a new piece of something to output using the same cout command, we have to put a set of double less-than symbols (<<) in before each of the pieces of something, like so:

```
cout << "first piece" << endl << "second";
```

We could have several pieces.

Notice also in Listing 2-2 that the second part of the first cout line and the next two cout lines all write their output on the same line. That's because there are no other endl words. The computer will simply continue writing where it left off when there is a new cout line with no endl.

You might try a few other combinations of words, <<'s, and endl's. Listing 2-3 shows one possibility:

Listing 2-3 Third HELLO.CPP

```
#include <iostream.h>
void main()
{
  cout << "The only reason" << endl;
  cout << "I'm doing" << endl << "this stupid" << endl;
  cout << "exercise" << endl << "...";
}
```

And, there's one more part of the program we've been ignoring, which we'll look at now: the first line.

```
#include <iostream.h>
```

The #include line tells the computer to use some parts of a program someone else wrote. This other program does stuff we need but don't have to worry about. In this case, the program we want, designated by "iostream.h" gives our program the ability to write lines of text on the screen. That is, it tells the computer how to do the cout thing (pronounced "see-out-thang").

Notice that this is in keeping with what Bill told us before he skipped town. The computer must be told how to do the things we want it to do, and cout is no exception. (Okay, so he didn't say *exactly* that. But when someone *leaves town,* he can't hear us slander him!)

So anyway, iostream.h tells the computer how to do the cout thing. And that frees us from having to worry about it. That's one nice thing about C and C++. There are lots of little things like the iostream (called libraries) that tell the computer how to do various things we don't want to have to waste our time worrying about.

Variables

Now we'll explore those things called *variables*, introduced in Chapter 1. Recall that a variable is a piece of computer memory that may be thought of like a line on a sheet of notebook paper. It consists of a type, a name, and possibly a value.

There are many different types available. The computer has several built in, and we can make our own, too. The most common type is integer, which is notated in C++ as int.

The name is simply for accessing the correct line on the sheet of notebook paper. We decide on the name ourselves, though, and it should be descriptive of the values that will be stored on that line.

For instance, suppose we want to tell the computer to set aside one line on its sheet of notebook paper as an integer, and this line is used for remembering the number of times the IRD has eaten today. We might call this variable *Eaten*, and it would be an integer. So we would have the following line in our program:

```
int Eaten;
```

The rule is that the type goes first, then the name, and then a semicolon.

Later on in the program, we might decide to store a number in this variable; that is, we might tell the computer to remember a certain number by putting it on the line on the imaginary sheet of notebook paper. Here's what we would type in our program if, for instance, we wanted to remember that the IRD has eaten twice:

```
Eaten = 2;
```

Listing 2-4, then, is a sample program you can type in and run on your computer.

Listing 2-4 Using a Variable-1

```
#include <iostream.h>
void main()
{
    int Eaten;
    Eaten = 1;
    cout << "IRD has eaten " << Eaten << " times." << endl;
    Eaten = 2;
    cout << "IRD has eaten " << Eaten << " times." << endl;
}
```

When you type in and run this program, you will see:

```
IRD has eaten 1 times.
IRD has eaten 2 times.
```

Expressions

It's fine that we can store things in these imaginary notebook lines called variables, but what if we want to use the information? For instance, what if the IRD needs to keep track of its inventory, and needs to do a little math, like add on the latest food it just picked up at the grocery store?

In that case, the IRD just does it. It adds on. Listing 2-5 shows how.

Listing 2-5 Using a Variable-2

```
#include <iostream.h>
void main()
{
    int FoodSupply;
    FoodSupply = 5;
    cout << "IRD starts with " << FoodSupply;
    cout << " pieces of food." << endl;
    FoodSupply = FoodSupply + 6;
```

```
cout << "After shopping, the supply is ";
cout << FoodSupply;
}
```

The strange notation

```
FoodSupply = FoodSupply + 6;
```

means the computer will take the value in the variable called FoodSupply, add 6, and put this new number it gets in the variable called *FoodSupply*. In other words, it adds 6 to *FoodSupply's* current value. When you type in and run this program, you will see the following:

> IRD starts with 5 pieces of food.
>
> After shopping, the supply is 11

When Bell labs originally developed C, which C++ is based on, the developers felt this notation of adding on was redundant. Why type in the word *FoodSupply* twice? Programmers hate typing, so they came up with an abbreviation. Here it is:

```
FoodSupply += 6;
```

means add 6 to whatever value's in *FoodSupply* and make the result the new value of *FoodSupply*.

Here are some other possibilities. The // precede comments to us, the readers of the program. We can type them into the computer, and the computer will simply ignore them when it performs our program.

```
FoodSupply -= 1;    // Take 1 away from FoodSupply
FoodSupply *= 2;    // Double FoodSupply.  The * means times.
FoodSupply /= 3;    // Divide FoodSupply by 3.
                    // The / means divided by.
```

We can also group expressions with parentheses, like this:

```
(FoodSupply + 1) / 2 // Add 1 and then divide by 2.
```

If you're interested, check out the Order of Operations rules in the following box.

ORDER OF OPERATIONS

C++ first evaluates things that are grouped by parentheses. It then evaluates things that are being multiplied and divided, from left to right. Next, it evaluates additions and subtractions.

continued on next page

continued from previous page

Example:

(5 + 3) / 2 * 5 + 6 – 12 / 4

The computer first does the stuff in parentheses, changing the expression to this:

8 / 2 * 5 + 6 – 12 / 4

Next, it does all multiplications and divisions from left to right, getting

4 * 5 + 6 – 12 / 4
20 + 6 – 12 / 4
20 + 6 – 3

Finally, it does the additions and subtractions from left to right:

26 – 3

And gets the final answer,

23

Variable Names

C++, like all computer languages, has too many rules. It gets flat-out annoying at times. Unfortunately, computers are really touchy about precision, so we have to be careful to follow the rules properly when we write programs.

And here's another bunch of rules—the rules for variable names. They're set off in the next box, should you decide to skip it and come back later when you really need it.

TOO MANY RULES

The rules for variable names vary from computer to computer, but generally they can be up to 32 characters. (Check your own compiler manual to be sure, though.) They must start with a letter, either capital or lowercase, or an _ underscore character. After that, there can be no spaces, but there can be any combination of digits, letters, and the _ underscore character. Note that C++ is case sensitive, so *APPLE* is a separate variable from *Apple*.

These are proper variable names:

APPLE
Apple
DogFood2
IRD_IS_GREAT
ABC_DEF123456

And these are wrong:

76TROMBONES   (Can't start with a digit!)
IRDS.ARE.COOL   (Can't have a period!)

Fortunately, your friendly compiler will give you an error message if you break any of these rules.

3
OOPS, THERE GOES AN UNIDENTIFIED FLYING OBJECT

Another day has begun at work, and we decide it's time to visit Linda Pavlov. We haven't been down to Engineering since Bill took off a couple of days ago.

We find Linda working in Bill's office, holding down the fort while he's gone. She tells us her job can wait, but the OOP development can't. She uses some colorful metaphors to describe her current feelings toward Bill, and mentions that the Big Boss feels even stronger. Bill's gonna be in for a big surprise when he gets back. For that matter, she points, out, we might be in for a surprise, too. Like getting Bill's job.

We decide this is a good time to learn a little more about object-oriented programming. Just in case.

Puttin' on the Ritz with a Little Class

Linda's still doing Bill's work of describing various parts of the dog, called objects, and giving them abilities, called methods, and attributes, which are values and lists of things. We wonder if we could possibly take a shot at it.

Her eyes light up and she says, "Oh yes, indeed! This is a wonderful opportunity for you!" (She tends to over-dramatize on occasion.) "Let's talk about the dog's internal energy supply!"

She stands up and approaches a conveniently located chalkboard, and writes some stuff on it:

Object: Energy Supply

She says, "We're going to create an object called Energy Supply."

"Wait," we say. "That's not an object."

"Sure it is. An object doesn't have to be something concrete."

"Ohhhhhhhkay."

"Really," she says. "An object can be any noun, whether concrete or not. Do you believe me?"

"I guess."

"Good enough. What are some of the methods for an energy supply?"

"Well, it doesn't do much. It must sit around, watching TV all day. Hahahahaha!"

She grins and says, "Very funny. Seriously, what are some of the methods?"

"What do you mean? The energy supply doesn't do anything."

"Sure it does. Does it remain the same all the time?"

"Well, no, ummm, it changes."

"Exactly! Changes how?"

"Exercise will make it go down, I guess."

"Correct! It can decrease! And just the same, it can . . ."

We don't like the way this is headed. We raise our hand sarcastically. "Ooh, ooh! Pick me! Pick me!"

She points to us.

"Increase!"

"Exactly!" The excitement in her voice is almost sickening. She writes the two things on the board.

Object: Energy Supply
Methods
Increase by a certain amount
Decrease by a certain amount

"Now," she says, "There's one thing we have to consider. When we create the object, we need an initial amount of energy, even if it's zero. How can we do that?"

"Well, we could have a method called *initialize*."

"Yup, and that's almost what we'll do. Except instead of saying it initializes the object, let's be more dramatic and for fun say it constructs the object. It fills in the details. It builds it. And in programming, the way you represent this Constructor method is by giving it the same name as the object. And we'll give it an initial amount as its parameter. She writes:

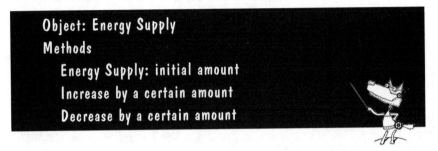

Object: Energy Supply
Methods
    Energy Supply: initial amount
    Increase by a certain amount
    Decrease by a certain amount

"Very good," she says. "And what are the attributes of the energy supply object?"

"Well, um, type of energy, I guess."

"Sure, that's one. But let's hold off on that for just a minute. What's another attribute?"

Suddenly it hits us. "How *much* energy! The level of energy!"

"Yes!" She adds more to the chalkboard.

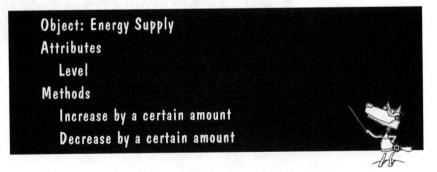

Object: Energy Supply
Attributes
    Level
Methods
    Increase by a certain amount
    Decrease by a certain amount

"Remember, we also need to look at how to implement these things."

"Let's skip that part," we say.

"Okay, but let's at least talk about it. How would you implement the constructor?"

"Well, the level needs to be set equal to the amount we're giving as the parameter to the constructor."

"Very good. And the increase and decrease methods?"

"For increase, we add to the level the amount to increase by, and for decrease we subtract from the level the amount to decrease by."

"Good. Let's move on now and look at the type of energy. This object we've created could, actually, represent one type of energy. Suppose the dog has two types of energy."

We remember a couple terms from school and decide to impress her. "Kinetic and potential."

Her eyes widen. "Wow! Ummm, I'm not sure I remember my physics. So let's make our two types of energy 'good' and 'bad.' Suppose the IRD has these two types of energy. Really, both types could be represented like the object here on the chalkboard, right? So let's say that what we've written on the board doesn't represent an actual energy object, but rather it represents all energy objects. It represents an entire classification of objects: energy. So instead let's call it a class of object, or just class." She erases the word "object" and writes the word "class."

```
Class: Energy Supply
Attributes
    Amount
Methods
    Increase by a certain amount
    Decrease by a certain amount
```

She continues. "When we have an individual object of classification, Energy Supply, we can safely say it's an object. But let's also say it's an instance of class Energy Supply."

"Instance? But that means—"

"I know what it normally means. But remember, we're computer programmers, so we have to take words we already know and give them definitions that have nothing to do with the original definition. That way others don't know what we're talking about, and it makes them feel inferior."

"I don't want to do that!"

She laughs. "I'm only joking! I figure since I'm in Bill's office, I have to act like Bill."

We laugh a little and decide it's time to get back to our office.

In an Instance, the Dog Had Class

After we arrive back at our office, we spend some time thinking about what Linda told us.

She mentioned classifying objects into groups called classes. Classes of objects. Let's see if we can think of another class of object.

We look at the IRD sitting on the floor. He's fully operational, yet he's just sort of staring off into space. We can't help but wonder what's on his dog mind.

Oh, yeah, engineering needs to fix our IRD's eyes. They're stuck open, yet he's sound asleep.

We wave our hands in front of his eyes. Wide open, yet he's totally unaware. We notice his eyes are sort of green. That's the color we had requested when we filled out the eye section of the form.

The form . . . Wait a minute! The *eye* could be considered a type of object, or a class, and the actual green eyes in this particular IRD could be two instances of the eye class! So that's what Linda was trying to say! And these eyes are green. Others could be brown, blue, yellow, orange, purple, whatever. They each have their own color. So color would be an attribute of the class eye.

We stand up and approach the chalkboard in our office. We never noticed we had a chalkboard before. It's as if life were just some sort of silly story and the author conveniently put it here.

Anyway, we try and remember what Linda wrote, only we'll write it for the class "eye." Here's what we write on the board.

```
Class: Eye
Attributes
    Color
Methods
```

Cool! Now lets add some methods. Let's see, they can look right, left, up, and down. So let's add those. Oh yeah, when we were in Chapter 1—er, two days ago, that is—Bill mentioned the eyes also need the ability to recognize food. So we'll include that, too. But what's the parameter? Food? No, because if the IRD already knows what the food is, he wouldn't need a method to recognize it. It seems the IRD needs an entire picture, and from there can identify the food. So that'll work.

And while we're at it, let's add some more attributes. Hmmm . . . How far the dog can see would be one. This is what we write:

```
Class: Eye
Attributes
    Color
    Sight Distance
Methods
    Look Up
    Look Down
    Look Right
    Look Left
    Recognize(picture)
```

What Goes into the Dog Must Come Out

The IRD starts barking and holds out his paw. We look at him questioningly, and realize he has an incoming call for us. We touch his paw, and can feel a strange pulse of energy coming into our fingers. It travels up our arms, into our neck, and right to our ears.

We hear a voice. The dog's communication device is operational! The voice is Linda Pavlov's.

"Hi!" she says. "Thought I'd try out the new communication device. Pretty sweet, wouldn't you say? Anyway, the reason I'm calling is to mention something about the methods. Think about the recognition method in the eyes."

We look at the chalkboard and wonder if she could possibly know what we wrote on it. Naw, purely coincidental.

She continues. "You've probably already figured out that the Recognize method requires a picture, and from there finds the piece of food in the picture, if there is any at all. Right?"

We look at the chalkboard and nod.

"This is like a telephone," she says, "and you can't just nod. You have to speak, because I can't see you."

"Yes!" we shout.

"Well, think of the method as a machine that has a function: It takes in a picture, finds the food, and spits out the name of the food. In other words, it takes a parameter, and spits out a result."

We envision a piece of food coming out of the IRD's eyes.

"What are you imagining?" she asks.

We tell her what we envisioned.

She laughs and says, "Well, actually, the computer inside the eye will send an electronic representation of the food's name to the main part of the brain. It doesn't actually send the food itself, just as the eye only looks at the picture, but doesn't actually take it in."

That makes sense. So when the eye performs the recognition method, it performs the function of looking at the picture, processing what it sees by finding the food, and sending the name of the food onto the brain. Interesting. We ask if all methods are like that.

She says, "Nope. Some methods don't really send back anything; that is, they don't return anything. They just do something like modify an attribute or tell another object to perform a method."

We thank her for this valuable piece of information and say good-bye. We're not sure how to hang up the IRD, but the IRD put his paw down, so apparently that did the trick.

So some of the methods perform a function of taking something in—a parameter—and possibly returning a result. Hmmm. Maybe that's what they mean by "function." A function is something that takes in a value and possibly returns a result.

Don't Panic

Linda reminds us not to panic. "There's been a lot to this chapter," she says.

We look around the room, trying to find this chapter thing she's referring to.

"But don't worry," she continues. "We don't need to memorize anything. Just so we've seen it once; then we can come back and review it again later!"

Here's what we've seen:

- building objects and methods
- constructors
- instance
- class

Program Section

We decide to try out some of this new class stuff. We sit down at our computer and break out the *IRD Programmer's Manual*, but it has no examples, so we dig through the bookshelf until we find a completely imaginary book with some good examples. It's called *Example Book for Simple C++*. Great! We open it up and, as it happens, the same example Linda was showing us is in this book. Imagine that!

First Class

The first example is a class of objects of type EnergyLevel. It consists of one attribute, called Level, and no methods.

Listing 3-1 is the complete program; you may type it in and run it.

Listing 3-1 EnergyLevel 1

```
#include <iostream.h>
class EnergyLevel
{
public:
    int Level;
};

void main ()
{
    EnergyLevel good;
    good.Level = 10;
    cout << "Good's energy level is at ";
    cout << good.Level << endl;
    good.Level ++;
    cout << "Good's energy level is now up to ";
    cout << good.Level << endl;
}
```

When we run it we see:

> Good's energy level is at 10
> Good's energy level is now up to 11

The *Example Book for Simple C++* has a pretty good description of the program. Here it is:

The first line tells the computer we need to do some input and output; that is, we're going to use commands for displaying things, in this case the cout command. The next line tells the computer we're going to describe to it a class called EnergyLevel. A class is only a description of a kind of object, so when we enter in a class as we did here, we're only telling the computer about the objects that will be of this class. We're not actually creating the objects themselves.

After the name of the class, the rest of the class description is enclosed in curly brackets. The final curly bracket of a class description is followed by a semicolon.

The first line inside the class description is the word "public." We won't worry too much about what it means just yet; but for now it suffices to say that the stuff that follows is accessible by every part of the program, not just methods within this class. (Of course, we don't even have any methods yet.)

The second line inside the class description, int Level;, is telling the computer that this class has an attribute that is of type integer and name Level.

And that's the whole class. It has one attribute, an integer called Level, and that attribute is accessible by the whole program.

Inside the main, the first line, EnergyLevel good, is where we actually create an object of type EnergyLevel. Since the computer does the stuff inside the main first, and proceeds step by step, this means we're telling the computer to create an object of type EnergyLevel before it does anything else. Like variables, we have to have first the type of object, the class name. In this case it's EnergyLevel. Next, we specify the name of this particular object. In this case, it's good.

So that means we are telling the computer to create an object called good of class EnergyLevel.

On the second line inside main, we are telling the computer to save a value in good's attribute called Level. This value we're giving it is 10. The rule for accessing the attributes is to give the name of the particular object, followed by a period, followed by the attribute name. Remember, each individual object gets its own attributes, and those attributes can differ from object to object, even if they are in the same class. So we must specify the particular object here, not simply the class.

The third and fourth lines tell the computer to print a message on the screen including the current value of good's attribute called Level.

On the fifth line, we're using the ++ notation (meaning "add 1") to tell the computer to increase good's Level attribute by 1, so it moves from 10 to 11.

And the sixth and seventh lines tell the computer to print another message on the screen.

The final line is the closing curly bracket for the code describing what main does. Remember, this one doesn't end with a semicolon.

(In case you're getting frustrated with the do's and don'ts about semicolons, see "The Final Word on Semicolons" in Chapter 13.)

Second Class

After looking over the program for a while and trying to understand what's happening, we decide we indeed do understand and we're ready for the next example.

The *Example Book* continues with the previous example by building on to it. We can see it added a single line to the class description of the class EnergyLevel, and it inserted some stuff immediately after the class description and before the main. It also added a couple of lines inside the main. Listing 3-2 is the example.

Listing 3-2 EnergyLevel 2

```
#include <iostream.h>
class EnergyLevel
{
public:
    int Level;
    void Drain()
    {    Level = 0;    }
};

void main ()
{
    EnergyLevel good;
    good.Level = 10;
    cout << "Good's energy level is at ";
    cout << good.Level << endl;
    good.Level ++;
    cout << "Good's energy level is now up to ";
    cout << good.Level << endl;
    good.Drain();
    cout << "Good's energy level has been drained to ";
    cout << good.Level << endl;
}
```

When run, this program puts the following on the screen:

```
Good's energy level is at 10
Good's energy level is now up to 11
Good's energy level has been drained to 0
```

We read some more in the *Example Book,* and can see that the line

```
void Drain();
```

tells the computer that this class is to have a single method called Drain().

In Chapter 1, during our discussion with Dr. Old, we found that many methods have to give back or return information to the part of the program that activated the method. When you have a method that does this, you have to specify the type of information it will return, such as int, just before the method name in the class description (that is, where the word "void" is, above). But many methods don't return anything. In this case, we would hope we could just not put anything before the function name, meaning nothing return. Unfortunately, that's not the case. Rather, we need to tell the computer to return nothing. The way we do that is with the word "void". So the line

```
void Drain()
```

means this class has a method called Drain, which takes no parameters (there's nothing inside the parentheses) and returns nothing.

So far, the code doesn't tell us or the computer what this method does. Ideally, the name should be descriptive, and indeed Drain is a method intended to drain all the energy, resetting Level to 0.

The lines after the class description tell the computer what to do when it executes the Drain method. Recall that in our discussion with Bill, we learned that we have to tell the computer not only *what* the method is, but *how* to do it.

Just as with main, we have a set of opening and closing curly braces with no semicolon at the end.

Inside these braces we describe to the computer what the method does. In this case it does one line of code,

```
level = 0;
```

which sets the level attribute to 0. Notice that in main we needed to specify the name of the object, good, before accessing the attributes. When we're inside the method descriptions, we don't need to do that. In fact, this method is for all objects of type EnergyLevel, so we really can't specify a particular object: It's for all objects of type EnergyLevel.

Third Class

Now that we're getting into the swing of things, let's put down the example book and proceed on our own. We'll add another method to the class. This method increases the energy level by a specified amount. It takes one parameter, the amount to increase the level by.

Listing 3-3 shows the class; the new parts are the line beginning with the word "Increase," and the method describing Increase. The main is also altered slightly to demonstrate the new method.

Listing 3-3 EnergyLevel 3

```
#include <iostream.h>
class EnergyLevel
{
public:
    int Level;
    void Drain()
    {    Level = 0;    }
    void Increase(int Amount)
    {    Level += Amount;    }
};

void main ()
{
    EnergyLevel good;
    good.Level = 10;
    cout << "Good's energy level is at ";
    cout << good.Level << endl;
    good.Increase(1);
    cout << "Good's energy level is now up to ";
    cout << good.Level << endl;
}
```

When we run this, we see the same thing as in the first example:

> Good's energy level is at 10
> Good's energy level is now up to 11

Notice one thing in particular here: The line that said

`good.Level++`

is now replaced by

`good.Increase(1);`

Basically, we've replaced a reference to the attribute with a call to a method. This is generally good practice. In another chapter we'll look more at the reasons for this, but for now let's just say that when we use the class, we shouldn't have to concern ourselves with the types of the attributes.

Fourth Class

We think about what was said in the last section, and decide to see what the *IRD Programmer's Manual* has to say. After the usual struggles of reading it, we find that it's good practice to make sure the parts of the program that use a class don't directly access the attributes. Rather, those parts of the program access them indirectly through the methods.

So what does this mean for our EnergyLevel class? It means we've already partly accomplished that goal: We've created a method that allows us to increase the level attribute. But we still need to be able to set the level initially and read it. How do we do that without directly accessing the attribute? Once again, we have to create a couple of methods.

The first method we create will be for setting the initial value of the Level attribute. We do this through what's known as a constructor. Recall from the discussion with Linda Pavlov that the constructor is the method that gets executed (that is, gets activated) right away when an object is created.

But when is an object created? In the examples above, the Good object gets created when the computer performs the line

```
EnergyLevel good;
```

So this is when the Constructor method gets called. But this particular class doesn't yet have a Constructor method; we have to add it. Listing 3-4 is the revised code with the Constructor method.

Listing 3-4 EnergyLevel 4

```
#include <iostream.h>
class EnergyLevel
{
public:
    int Level;
    EnergyLevel(int InitialAmount)
    {    Level = InitialAmount;    }
    void Drain()
    {    Level = 0;    }
    void Increase(int Amount)
    {    Level += Amount;    }
};

void main ()
{
    EnergyLevel good(5);
    cout << "Good's energy level starts at ";
    cout << good.Level << endl;
    good.Level = 10;
    cout << "Good's energy level is at ";
    cout << good.Level << endl;
```

```
    good.Increase(10);
    cout << "Good's energy level is now up to ";
    cout << good.Level << endl;
}
```

The output of this program (that is, the stuff you see on the screen when you run the program) looks like this:

Good's energy level starts at 5
Good's energy level is at 10
Good's energy level is now up to 20

Notice a few things about the constructor. First, it doesn't return a type, not even void. If that seems strange, don't worry—it is. Returning void means returning nothing. But it's just another annoying rule that we have to get used to. The constructor doesn't have anything before it, no void, no nothing. It's not allowed to.

Notice also how the constructor gets called. When the computer executes the first line in the main,

```
EnergyLevel good(5)
```

it calls the constructor with the parameter 5. So the first thing that happens here is that the constructor gets called with a parameter 5, and the level is set to the value of 5.

Fifth Class

Here's the final revision to our class. We said above that there are two things needed, and we did the first, a constructor. Now we need a method for accessing the Level attribute. We'll call it GetLevel. It takes no parameters, and returns an integer.

We'll also make one more revision: Recall that in Chapter 2 we noticed the word "void" before the word "main," and observed that this means we're not returning anything to the computer. Here, we'll do something a bit different, and return something. We're only allowed to return an integer to the computer. Unfortunately, for many computers, the returned integer often isn't used. The general idea is that if we return a number other than 0 to the computer, it means something went wrong, and the computer should be told. For instance, if we're writing a program that causes the IRD to save his name to a disk file, and the file runs out of room, we would return an error number to the computer. The computer may then display a warning message to the user that there was an error, but some systems don't. Really, though, the program itself should display the message, anyway. So most of the programs in *Simple C++* will not return anything to the computer.

Listing 3-5 is the final revision to the class.

Listing 3-5 EnergyLevel 5

```
#include <iostream.h>
class EnergyLevel
{
public:
    int Level;
    EnergyLevel(int InitialAmount)
    {    Level = InitialAmount;    }
    void Drain()
    {    Level = 0;    }
    void Increase(int Amount)
    {    Level += Amount;    }
    int GetLevel()
    {    return Level;    }
};

int main ()
{
    EnergyLevel good(10);
    cout << "Good's energy level is at ";
    cout << good.GetLevel() << endl;
    good.Increase(10);
    cout << "Good's energy level is now up to ";
    cout << good.GetLevel() << endl;

    // Return a 0 to the computer.  You may want to try
    // changing the 0 here to something like 100
    // and see if your computer even does
    // anything.

    return 0;
}
```

The output of this program is:

Good's energy level is at 10
Good's energy level is now up to 20

And that's it! We now have a class that allows us to initialize its attribute, change it, and read it, without directly accessing it. We used a constructor to initialize it, and we used methods to change it, and access it. Notice the main never used the attribute Level. It only calls EnergyLevel's methods. Believe it or not, that's good!

And, that's probably more than enough OOP for today (er, this chapter). Might be a good time for another pizza break. . . .

Part 2
Dog Talk and Other Useful Languages (Like C++)

4

DRIVING
ON THE LOOP

It's another day at PETT, and we're sitting in our cubicle when the phone rings. It's B.B., the Big Boss.

"Hello," roars B.B.'s stereotypically deep baritone voice.

"Hi," we say. "How's the missus?" we predictably ask.

"Fine, fine. Thanks for asking. Reason I'm calling, Bill down in Engineering has disappeared, we'd like you to take his place."

"Great!"

"Good, good. Glad to hear it, glad to hear it. You'll be starting with Linda Pavlov. Deal? Deal. Good. Now get to work down there. You'll take over Bill's office so Linda can get back to her own job. Got it? Good. If not, then get it. Now get down there already!"

We hang up the phone, and enter a message into the terminal requesting our IRD to gather up our things and bring them downstairs. He looks slightly confused.

"Oh, yeah," we say. "I forgot. The only physical things you're programmed to do are chase firetrucks, eat, and clean. Well, then, send a message to the movers asking them to move my stuff. Got it? Good. Now get down there already!"

We head downstairs, and begin work on the OOP.

Entering the Loop

That afternoon, we're hard at work on building the next generation of the IRD.

We've been carefully describing how to do each method in our classes of objects, and we stumbled across something interesting.

Every method performs its stuff in a step-by-step fashion, one step followed by the next.

But there's a problem. We've been working on the class for the Mouth object, and particularly the Eat method. To perform the Eat method, the mouth still works step by step, eating one piece of food after another. But how do we program this? We could give a command in our method to eat a single piece of food. We could follow that with another command telling the mouth to eat a second piece of food. Then another command for a third piece of food. But what if there are only two pieces? Or what if there are 3,000?

We might consider having separate methods, one for the situation where there's one piece of food, one for the situation where there are two pieces, and so on. But that would be a pain in the IRD's butt!

Wouldn't it be nice if we could simply tell the IRD to repeat the same step of eating a single piece of food until the food's gone?

Maybe we'd better call in the Resident Genius.

Repeat What the Genius Says

Linda Pavlov enters the room. "My IRD told me you called?"

"We got trouble," we say. "We need to tell the IRD to do something over and over."

"What exactly must it do over and over?"

"Eat pieces of food."

"And how long should it keep munching?"

"As long as there's food left."

Linda approaches the chalkboard and begins to write. "So what we need to do is this:"

```
Do-While construct
Do the following:
    Eat a piece of food
while there's food left
```

"Exactly!" we say.

"No problem. The computer can do just that. It's called the *do-while* construct."

We ignore that last phrase.

She continues, "We can program the computer to repeat any set of steps over and over as long as a certain condition is met."

We ask her for another example.

"Sure!" she says. "Let's say we're operating our IRD in communication mode, and we give it a whole bunch of messages to send out. Later, it begins sending out the messages. This involves doing the same thing over and over—it repeats the step of sending a message. It does this over and over until what happens?"

"As long as there are messages."

"Exactly. We could write it like this:"

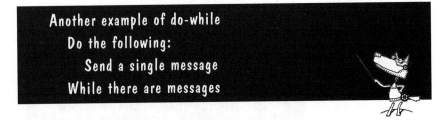

Another example of do-while
Do the following:
    Send a single message
While there are messages

She adds, "There are lots and lots of times where this is needed. But there are other ways we can express the same concept. Let's have a new section header, though."

Looping Back for More Dogfood

Linda continues talking. "When the computer does something over and over, it's called a *loop*."

"A loop? But a loop is something that goes round and round, like a racetrack."

"Exactly. And in computers, a loop is something the computer does over and over. And there are a few different ways we can tell the computer to do something over and over. Let's look at the first example again, the one about eating dog food. We can tell the computer to use the do-while construct, as we did above. Or we could express it in a very similar

way, only a tad different, like this: While there is still more dog food, eat a piece. We'd write it this way:

```
While construct
    While there is still more dogfood
        Eat a piece
end-while
```

"The computer will know that it needs to do the 'eat a piece' part over and over while there's still more dog food; and when there's no more, it will proceed to the part of the program that comes after the while loop."

"So what's the difference between the do-while and the while constructs?" we ask.

"The do-while construct does something, and then tests if it should do it again. So it always does it at least once. The while construct, on the other hand, first tests if it should do it, and if not, it skips the thing entirely. So with the while construct, it may not even do the thing once."

We decide that we'll have to let that soak in a little bit. The Program Section should help because we can see some actual examples.

"Another way to express all this," she continues, "is to say, 'For each piece of dog food, eat that piece.' We'd write it like this:

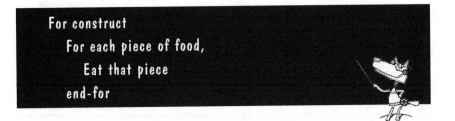

```
For construct
    For each piece of food,
        Eat that piece
    end-for
```

"Again, the computer will do the loop for each piece of dog food, and when there are no more pieces of dog food, the computer will proceed with the program after the loop. Does that make sense?"

"Sure. But it looks like with the for construct, you need to know in advance how many pieces there are."

"Exactly. And that's when you generally use the for construct: when you know how many times in advance you want to do the loop. So we have three constructs so far. Let's list them on the chalkboard."

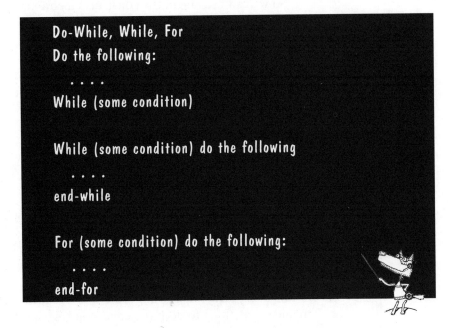

```
Do-While, While, For
Do the following:
    . . . .
While (some condition)


While (some condition) do the following
    . . . .
end-while


For (some condition) do the following:
    . . . .
end-for
```

Linda continues to talk some more, but we aren't able to comprehend her due to the rumbling in our stomach. "Have you had lunch?" we ask her.

"No, and I hear you haven't either. Shall we go grab a bite?"

"Sure. But let's leave the puppy chow here." We imagine applause at our sitcom-like remark. But Linda simply groans and forgets we ever said it. Maybe we weren't meant to be comedians.

Daydreaming

After lunch, we're back in our office, and Linda's talking some more. After a few minutes, we decide to start listening.

"Remember in Chapter 2, when we looked at expressions?"

We remind her that that was in the programming section, and that we skipped that part of the book.

"Well, in that case we won't go into heavy detail. But let's touch on it slightly. Suppose you're writing the eye's method for finding food. You need to scan through everything in the room, looking for food, right?"

"Sounds good."

"So we can use one of the constructs mentioned above, right?"

"Sure. We could say, 'For each thing in the room, see if it's a piece of food.'"

"Right! So suppose you find that it's a piece of food. Then you need to tell the brain. But how do you get the computer to tell the brain about the food, not for every object it finds, but the objects that are food?"

We think about the different constructs from earlier on, but can't come up with a method.

"You need to make a comparison. For each thing, see if it's a piece of food. And if so, then tell the brain. In other words:

```
For each thing in the room, do the following:
    if it's a piece of food,
        tell the brain.
    end-if
end-for
```

She adds, "The line starting with 'if' is the if construct. We could also include something to do if the condition isn't satisfied; that is, if it's not a piece of food. Suppose we want it to throw away anything that's not a piece of food. This is what we would do:

```
For each thing in the room, do the following:
    if it's a piece of food,
        tell the brain,
```

```
    else
        throw it away.
    end-if
end-for
```

"There are a few things you should realize about the comparisons, though," she says. "In an if construct, a comparison always takes place, and this often involves numbers. In the case of numbers, you can do all the kinds of comparison you can do in real life. You can say, 'If this number is equal to that?' Or you might say, 'If this number is greater than that number?' And so on. You might also say something like, 'If this number times 2 divided by 3 is equal to 532, then do such-and-such.' The computer can do all the math for you, so you don't have to. Most people like that idea!"

"Okay, okay. But why is this section called 'daydreaming'?"

"Because if the author called it 'math,' nobody would read it!"

"You got that right!"

"And most people start dozing off at the very mention of the M-word."

. . .

She talks some more about math, but we're losing interest. We start thinking about what we're gonna do this weekend. Maybe take the IRD out to the beach. We wonder if he can go in the water. Did the designers make him waterproof? Maybe he can float. Maybe he'll sink. That would be pretty devastating, having to spend the rest of eternity at the bottom of the ocean. Of course, the IRD would probably consider it a learning experience, examining the ocean floor and all the forms of plants and animals. We picture ourselves floating around at the bottom of the ocean, taking in the beautiful scenery . . .

"Wake up!"

"Huh?"

It's Linda Pavlov. "I told you that people doze off, and sure enough, you did!"

"I don't want to learn about math!"

She sighs and smiles. "Okay, okay, we'll put the rest in the code section, so you can skip it if you want. But first, let's see what you've learned today!"

Don't Panic

We've seen a lot of stuff in this chapter, so we may want to plan on reviewing it later on. Here's what we've seen:

- loops
- do-while loops
- while loops
- for loops
- if

Program Section

After Linda leaves, we begin playing with some of the constructs. We dig out the *Example Book for Simple C++,* and find lots of examples. First it has some examples of expressions, and then it has some examples of the constructs using expressions to test for things. Here they are.

Example 1: Integer Expressions

The first example (Listing 4-1) is just another example from what was covered in Chapter 2. It demonstrates some integer expressions.

Listing 4-1 Integer Expressions

```
#include <iostream.h>
void main()
{
    int Boring;
    int Example;

    Boring = 10;
    Boring++ ;
    cout << "Boring++ = " << Boring << endl;

    Example = (Boring + 4) / 2;
    cout << "(Boring + 4) / 2 = " << Example << endl;
}
```

The output of this program is:

```
Boring++ = 11
(Boring + 4) / 2 = 7
```

Recall that Boring++ means "add one to Boring." So when Boring starts at 10, and the computer does Boring++, Boring becomes 11.

Next, when the computer calculates Example, it adds 4 to Boring, to get 15, and then divides by 2. Since the answer to 15 divided by 2 is 7.5, which is not a whole number, the computer truncates it (removes the decimal part) to get 7. So that's what Example becomes.

Example 2: Floating Point Expressions

Often in programming we need to use numbers other than just integers. For instance, suppose our IRD needs to keep track of the distance covered after chasing a firetruck. Let's make a new class called Chase, with an attribute, DistanceTraveled, and a method called RanMore. The RanMore method takes a value for how far the IRD just ran, and this method adds that number to the DistanceTraveled attribute.

We could probably just use whole numbers, but it might be nice to keep track of more precise distances. To do this we use decimal numbers, which computer people like to call "floating point." (The reason for this name is this form of number need not have a fixed number of digits after the decimal point; rather than being fixed, the decimal point can "float.") Note that to use floating point numbers, you may need to set some special options in your C++ compiler. Check with the manual or a reliable friend to be sure. Now let's look at Listing 4-2.

Listing 4-2 Floating Point Expression

```
#include <iostream.h>

class Chase
{
    float DistanceTraveled;
public:
    Chase()    //Constructor:  Initialize DistanceTraveled.
        {  DistanceTraveled = 0.0;  }
    void RanMore(float HowFar)
        {  DistanceTraveled+= HowFar;  }
    float GetDistance()
        {  return DistanceTraveled;  }
};

void main()
{
```

continued on next page

continued from previous page

```
Chase Today;
Today.RanMore(10.5);
cout << "Ran 10.5 more miles!" << endl;
cout << "Total miles ran is " << Today.GetDistance() << endl;

Today.RanMore(5.3);
cout << "Ran another 5.3 miles!" << endl;
cout << "Total miles ran is " << Today.GetDistance() << endl;

cout << "Now for some goofy math!" << endl;
cout << "Distance is " << Today.GetDistance() << endl;
cout << "Distance times 2.6 is ";
cout << Today.GetDistance() * 2.6 << endl;
cout << "Distance divided by 2.6 is ";
cout << Today.GetDistance() / 2.6 << endl;
}
```

The output of this program looks like this:

```
Ran 10.5 more miles!
Total miles ran is 10.5
Ran another 5.3 miles!
Total miles ran is 15.8
Now for some goofy math!
Distance is 15.8
Distance times 2.6 is 41.08
Distance divided by 2.6 is 6.076923
```

Notice that when we create the object Today in the first line of main, the computer performs the constructor, which sets the DistanceTraveled attribute to 0.0. Next, when we call the RanMore method with the parameter 10.5, the computer adds 10.5 to the DistanceTraveled attribute, making it 10.5.

Later, we call the RanMore method a second time, only with 5.3 for the parameter. This adds 5.3 to the current value in DistanceTraveled, 10.5, to get 15.8.

Toward the end of the main method, we do some math on the DistanceTraveled attribute, basically just to see what happens. First we see what DistanceTraveled times 2.6 is, without changing DistanceTraveled; and then we see what DistanceTraveled divided by 2.6 is.

Example 3: Do-While Construct

Let's continue with the program in Example 2. We'll use the same class, but a new main. This example, Listing 4-3, uses a lot of variables in the main, so watch carefully. Also notice that at the end of the do-while loop we have to manually add 1 to the variable *Count*. If we don't do that, the program will run either forever, or until the world ends, or until the computer dies, or until we shut the computer off. (Some computers have a "break" mechanism, which lets you press a certain combination of keys to stop the program. Check your manual for details.)

Listing 4-3 Do-While Construct

```
#include <iostream.h>

class Chase
{
    float DistanceTraveled;
public:
    Chase()     //Constructor:  Initialize DistanceTraveled.
        { DistanceTraveled = 0.0;  }
    void RanMore(float HowFar)
        { DistanceTraveled+= HowFar;  }
    float GetDistance()
        { return DistanceTraveled;  }
};

void main()
{
    Chase AnotherChase;
    int Count;
    float LittleFarther;

    Count = 0;
    do
    {
        cout << "Enter distance ran...";
        cin >> LittleFarther;
        AnotherChase.RanMore(LittleFarther);
        Count++;
    } while (Count <= 3);
    cout << endl;
    cout << "We've run " << AnotherChase.GetDistance();
    cout << " miles." << endl;
}
```

When you run this program, the output will look something like this, depending on what numbers your enter in after the prompt "Enter distance ran."

> Enter distance ran...1.2
> Enter distance ran...2.3
> Enter distance ran...3.4
> Enter distance ran...4.5
>
> We've run 11.4 miles.

A common problem is getting the computer to do the loop precisely the number of desired times. Notice here that we started the *Count* at 0, and did it while *Count* is less than or equal to 3. This means it did it for *Count* = 0, *Count* = 1, *Count* = 2, and *Count* = 3, for a total of 4 times.

But the story would change slightly if we replace the line

```
} while (Count <= 3);
```

with

```
} while (Count < 3);
```

You might think about how this will change the number of iterations, and then try it yourself to see if you were right.

Example 4: While Construct

Listing 4-4 is the same example again, only with the while construct.

Listing 4-4 While Construct

```
#include <iostream.h>

class Chase
{
    float DistanceTraveled;
public:
    Chase()    //Constructor:  Initialize DistanceTraveled.
        { DistanceTraveled = 0.0;  }
    void RanMore(float HowFar)
        { DistanceTraveled+= HowFar;  }
    float GetDistance()
        { return DistanceTraveled;  }
};
```

```
void main()
{
    Chase AnotherChase;
    int Count;
    float LittleFarther;

    Count = 0;
    while (Count <= 3)
    {
        cout << "Enter distance ran...";
        cin >> LittleFarther;
        AnotherChase.RanMore(LittleFarther);
        Count++;
    }
    cout << endl;
    cout << "We've run " << AnotherChase.GetDistance();
    cout << " miles." << endl;
}
```

Notice that we don't have a keyword that specifies the end of the while loop, as we used in the text. Rather, in C++, the end of the while loop is denoted by the closing curly bracket, }.

Here's the output of this program, using the same data as in the previous example.

```
Enter distance ran...1.2
Enter distance ran...2.3
Enter distance ran...3.4
Enter distance ran...4.5

We've run 11.4 miles.
```

Notice it's the same as in the previous example. However, there's one big difference. With the do-while loop, the statements inside the loop will always get executed at least once, even if the condition fails. That's because the computer first performs the statements, then tests the condition. However, with the while loop, as in this example, you can code it so the statements inside the loop will never get executed, simply by making the condition something that will never occur, such as while (count > 0).

Example 5: For Construct

The for construct may be one of the most popular. Listing 4-5 is the same example again, only modified for the for construct. Notice the format of the for construct. There are three sets of things that go inside the parentheses after the word for.

The first thing is the initialization. In this case, we're setting *Count* to 0. This is what happens at the very beginning of the for loop.

The second thing is the condition. This is the condition under which the loop *continues to run*. Note that the loop ends when this condition is *no longer true*.

The third thing is the expression describing what happens after each iteration of the loop. In this case, after each iteration of the loop, *Count* is increased by 1.

Listing 4-5 For Construct

```
#include <iostream.h>

class Chase
{
    float DistanceTraveled;
public:
    Chase()      //Constructor:  Initialize DistanceTraveled.
        {  DistanceTraveled = 0.0;  }
    void RanMore(float HowFar)
        {  DistanceTraveled+= HowFar;  }
    float GetDistance()
        {  return DistanceTraveled;  }
};

void main()
{
    Chase AnotherChase;
    int Count;
    float LittleFarther;

    for (Count = 0; Count <= 3; Count = Count + 1)
    {
        cout << "Enter distance ran...";
        cin >> LittleFarther;
        AnotherChase.RanMore(LittleFarther);
    }
    cout << endl;
    cout << "We've run " << AnotherChase.GetDistance();
    cout << " miles." << endl;
}
```

You can probably guess the output:

```
Enter distance ran...1.2
Enter distance ran...2.3
Enter distance ran...3.4
Enter distance ran...4.5

We've run 11.4 miles.
```

As with the while loop, it's possible to set up the for loop so the computer never executes the statements inside the loop. Again, the way to do it is to make the condition something that's already not true, such as

```
for (Count = 0; Count < 0 ; Count = Count + 1)
```

In this case, *Count* is not less than 0, so the computer won't even do what's inside the loop. With the for loop, the computer will do what's inside the loop while the condition is true. In the case of Listing 4-5, that means while *Count* <= 3.

Example 6: If Construct

We can make lots of comparisons. The "equals" comparison is one.

Take a look at Listing 4-6. Notice that there's some strange notation here. It's the double equal sign, ==. C++ uses it to test if two things are equal. A single equal sign, =, on the other hand, is used for storing values in variables and attributes. A double equal sign, ==, as we have here, is a test for equality. Note that if you forget to use the double equal sign, ==, in a comparison such as the one in this example, the compiler *might not give you an error*. So be careful!

Listing 4-6 also demonstrates the less-than and greater-than comparisons, and the box after this example lists more comparisons.

Listing 4-6 If Construct

```
#include <iostream.h>
void main()
{
    int TestNumber;
    cout << "Enter the number of dog food pieces eaten" << endl;
```

continued on next page

continued from previous page

```
cin >> TestNumber;
if (TestNumber == 10)
{
    cout << "I ate just enough!" << endl;
}
if (TestNumber < 10)
{
    cout << "I didn't quite eat enough!" << endl;
}
if (TestNumber > 10)
{
    cout << "I feel sick.  I think I ate too much." << endl;
}
}
```

Here's the output of the program. It was run three times, each time with a different number entered:

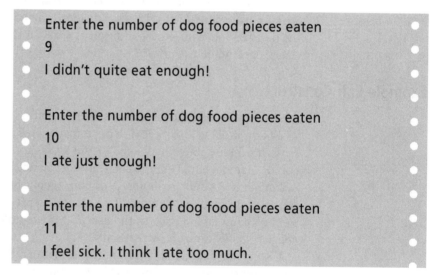

Enter the number of dog food pieces eaten
9
I didn't quite eat enough!

Enter the number of dog food pieces eaten
10
I ate just enough!

Enter the number of dog food pieces eaten
11
I feel sick. I think I ate too much.

Notice the format of the If statement. The word "if" is followed by a condition that must be in parentheses. The code to perform if the condition succeeds follows, and is surrounded by curly brackets. (Note that if we only have one line of code in the block of code following the If statement, as we do here, we need not surround it with curly brackets. However, it's generally advisable for readability.)

Example 7: Case Construct: A Super-If Statement

There's one more construct, and it wasn't covered in the text. Suppose you have a program to be run in the IRD's security mode, and this program asks for the IRD's serial number and returns the access level for entering a top-secret building. Access levels may be 0 for no access, 1 for regular access, and 2 for high-security access. The cases are

- If the serial number is 100, access level 2 is granted.

- If the serial number is 135, access level 1 is granted.

- If the serial number is any other number, access level 0 is granted.

Listing 4-7 is one possible program for accomplishing the task. Note that for a large computer system, the list of serial numbers and access codes would actually be stored in a disk file, and a program would scan through the disk file to get the proper access code. But when we only have a few serial numbers, this method works okay.

Listing 4-7 First Case Construct

```
#include <iostream.h>

void main()
{
    int SerialNumber;

    cout << "Enter the IRD's serial number. " << endl;
    cin >> SerialNumber;
```

continued on next page

continued from previous page

```
if (SerialNumber == 100)
{
    cout << "Access level 2 granted." << endl;
}
else if (SerialNumber == 135)
{
    cout << "Access level 1 granted." << endl;
}
else
{
    cout << "Access level 0: No entry allowed!" << endl;
}
}
```

Here's the output, again after three separate runs:

```
Enter the IRD's serial number.
135
Access level 1 granted.

Enter the IRD's serial number.
100
Access level 2 granted.

Enter the IRD's serial number.
110
Access level 0: No entry allowed!
```

Notice the format again. The condition for the If statement is in parentheses, and the code to perform if the condition is true follows. Next is the else block, and an optional If statement follows. Then comes a block of code surrounded by curly brackets.

When the computer runs this program, the first thing it does is the first two lines. Next it checks to see if SerialNumber is 100. If so, it prints the line "Access level 2 granted." Then it skips to the piece of code following the final else block in this large if construct. (In this case, it goes to the end of the program and finishes.)

If, however, the SerialNumber isn't 100, the computer skips to the first else line, and checks if SerialNumber is 135. If so, it prints the line "Access level 1 granted." Then it skips to the end of the last else block.

But if the SerialNumber isn't 135, it performs the stuff inside the final else block regardless. This means it prints the line "Access level 0: No entry allowed!" The program then ends.

This works well, but C++ provides an alternate approach. It's called the Switch statement. (In other computer languages, it's often called a Case statement.) Listing 4-8 is a quick example of the Switch statement.

Listing 4-8 Switch Statement

```
#include <iostream.h>

void main()
{
    int SerialNumber;

    cout << "Enter the IRD's serial number. " << endl;
    cin >> SerialNumber;
    switch (SerialNumber)
    {
        case 100:
            cout << "Access level 2 granted." << endl;
            break;
        case 135:
            cout << "Access level 1 granted." << endl;
            break;
        default:
            cout << "Access level 0: No entry allowed!" << endl;
            break;
    }
}
```

If we run this program three times, and use the same input as the previous listing, we see the same output as before:

```
Enter the IRD's serial number.
135
Access level 1 granted.

Enter the IRD's serial number.
100
Access level 2 granted.

Enter the IRD's serial number.
110
Access level 0: No entry allowed!
```

The computer follows essentially the same steps here.

The rules for the Switch statement are: The variable whose value is being tested goes in parentheses after the Switch statement, and a block of code enclosed in curly brackets follows. The block of code consists of a set of Case statements, as shown in this example. Each case line ends with a colon, and the code to be performed for that particular case follows. Notice that the code for each case ends with the word "break." Break tells the computer to immediately exit the construct it's currently working on, whether it's a while, for, do-while, or switch construct. In this example, the computer will jump to the end of the switch block when the break is encountered. If we don't have it here, the computer will continue on to the code following the next case.

For example, try removing the break after Case 100: in the example above. When we have the situation where SerialNumber equals 100, the computer will do the line

```
cout << "Access level 2 granted." << endl;
```

and continue on to the next case, and do the line

```
cout << "Access level 1 granted." << endl;
```

Occasionally, we may want the computer to step into the next case, but not this time. Hence we need the Break statement.

So when do you use the switch construct rather than the if construct? When you have a single variable that has to be compared to a whole bunch of values, and different tasks need to be performed for each situation—for each case. If you're only comparing something to two values, then an If statement will often do. But really, it's up to you. You can use either, and some people prefer one or the other.

Example 8: More Ifs

Sometimes you may want your IRD to do something only when two conditions are true. Or sometimes you may want it to do something if either of two conditions are true. For example, you may want it to be either asleep or awake, or you may want it to pant when running or walking.

Let's say you want to have a program print a message if both of two numbers are less than 10—that is, only print the message if both the first is less than 10 *and* the second is less than 10. This is known as the AND operator.

On the other hand, you may want to have a program print a message if either of two numbers are less than 10. If the first is less than 10, or the second is less than 10 (or both are) then print the message. This is known as the OR operator.

Listing 4-9 demonstrates this.

Listing 4-9 IF, AND, and OR

```cpp
#include <iostream.h>

#define FILENAME "4-8c.cpp"
#include "output.h"
void main()
{
    int First, Second;
    cout << "Enter 1st" << endl;
    cin >> First;

    cout << "Enter 2nd" << endl;
    cin >> Second;

    // AND operator
    if (First < 10 && Second < 10)
    {
    cout << "Both are less than 10";
    cout << endl << endl;
    }

    // OR operator
    if (First < 10 || Second < 10)
    {
    cout << "At least one is less than 10,";
    cout << " maybe both are." << endl << endl;
    }
{
```

Notice we use the && for the AND operator. The first If statement means "If First is less than 10 *and* Second is less than 10, do the following." The second If statement means, "If First is less than 10 or Second is less than 10, do the following."

Here's the output if we enter the numbers 5 and 6 for First and Second, respectively:

```
Enter 1st
5
Enter 2nd
6
Both are less than 10
At least one is less than 10, maybe both are.
```

Notice in the first If statement the computer checks if First is less than 10 (which it is) *and* if Second is less than 10 (which it is). It then prints the message. In the second If statement, it checks if either is less than 10. Since both qualify here, it prints this message, too. (It's important to realize that the OR operator can succeed if both conditions work, as in this case.)

Here's the output if we enter the numbers 5 and 12 for First and Second, respectively:

```
Enter 1st
5
Enter 2nd
12
At least one is less than 10, maybe both are.
```

Notice this time, First is less than 10, but Second isn't. Since we can't say "5 is less than 10 and 15 is less than 10," without lying, the computer doesn't print the message after the first If statement. However, for the second If statement, either or both condition can be true. The first one is (5 is indeed less than 10), so the computer prints the message for the second If statement.

Now here's the output if we enter the numbers 12 and 13 for First and Second, respectively:

```
Enter 1st
12
Enter 2nd
13
```

The computer didn't print either message, because in the first If statement, we can't say both are less than 10, and in the second If statement, we can't say either is less than 10.

We can also have more than two conditions; for instance we could check if three conditions are all under 10 by putting another && followed by a third condition, say Third < 10.

A Million Ideas

There are lots of possible examples for demonstrating the different constructs. You might try adjusting the conditions in Examples 3, 4, and 5, to see if you can get the computer to do the loop just once. Then see if you can adjust the conditions to get it to not do the loop at all. (In some of the cases, it may not be possible!)

You might also try to modify the case example in Example 7 so that two serial numbers, 100 and 101, both have Access Level 2. This requires either adding another case, or replacing the line

```
case 100:
```

with the line

```
case 100: case 101:
```

Bearing in mind what was mentioned about the Break statement, above, see if you can understand why this approach works.

5
INHERITING A MILLION-DOLLAR DOG

Big Boss sounded like he wanted everything done yesterday, so it's time to buckle down. Today we decide to organize our work. As we look at our IRD, we realize that he's made up of lots and lots of objects, each being a certain type or class. (Remember, class is another word for "type" or "kind," and object is the actual thing.) Some objects are the same class, and the only difference between these objects is that they have different values in their attributes.

Doganatomy

For instance, we see in Bill's notes that the HindLeg class describes the objects that make up the hind legs. These hind legs are nearly identical, except that one is the left and one is the right. So the HindLeg class has an attribute called WhichSide, and this attribute is set to "left" if the object is a left leg, and "right" if the object is a right leg. Other than the differences in attribute values, these objects of class HindLeg are all the same. In fact, the same is true for all objects that belong to a common class.

Sometimes, objects need to have different methods. To see this, we look through the section in Bill's notes about the legs. At first, he created a class called Leg and decided to create four objects of this class Leg, and simply vary the attributes. But he ran into a problem. The front

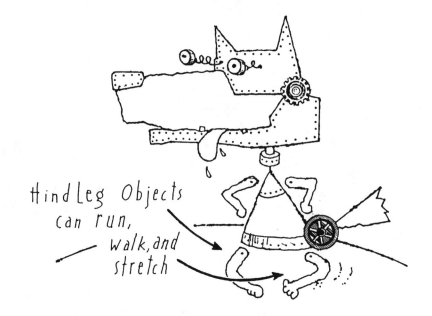

Hind Leg Objects can run, walk, and stretch

legs have a lot of abilities in common with the hind legs, but the front legs have some abilities the back legs lack, and vice versa. For instance, the front legs can walk, run, and stretch, as can the hind legs. But the front legs can kick, while the hind legs can't. The back legs can support the IRD on only two feet, while the front legs can't.

So how did Bill implement this?

He created a class, called Leg, and gave it methods for the basic Leg abilities: Run, Walk, and Stretch. He also included a WhichLeg attribute, which takes on the value of either left or right. Let's copy Bill's notes onto the chalkboard:

```
Class Leg
Attributes:
    WhichLeg
Methods
    Run
    Walk
    Stretch
```

But this class is too general. It's not good enough for the front legs, nor the hind legs. So Bill had to create a couple of new classes, one called FrontLeg and one called HindLeg. The two Front Leg objects are each of class FrontLeg, and the two HindLeg objects are each of class HindLeg.

Each of these two classes of objects has the abilities to run, walk, and stretch, so Bill used a trick to save typing: He created the original Leg class, and then created two new classes, FrontLeg and HindLeg, which (he wrote in his notes) are "derived" from the first class, Leg.

We check the *IRD Programmer's Manual* to see what it says about deriving classes. Apparently, when we create a class, we can do what's known as *derive* new classes from this first. In other words, we can create a new class of objects that gets all the same attributes and methods as the original *base class* of objects. From there we're free to modify any of the methods in the newly derived class, or we can add new methods and attributes.

We try to relate this strange concept to the classes for the legs. The first class, Leg, has methods Run, Walk, Stretch. Bill then derived two new classes, FrontLeg and HindLeg, from this class Leg. This means the two classes, FrontLeg and HindLeg, automatically get Run, Walk, and Stretch methods, along with the attribute WhichLeg. That is, these derived classes *inherit* the methods and attributes of the base class.

But why did he do that? It seems he wanted to save typing. Why type in the same methods for two classes, when we could type it in once for one class and derive two classes from this first? It saves typing. It's a way of reusing code.

But more than that, it looks like if he wants to change something in one of these inherited methods, he only has to change it in the base class. And the derived class will inherit the changes. This saves the trouble of rewriting and retesting the code. And beyond that, it also helps organize the code. The general code for all the derived classes goes in the base class, and the derived classes get this general code. Then the derived classes add more specific code for their specific situation.

Figure 5-1 shows a diagram demonstrating this concept. Notice the two derived classes, HindLeg and FrontLeg, automatically get all the same methods and attributes as their base class, Leg. That is, the classes HindLeg and FrontLeg *inherited* all the same methods and attributes.

The *IRD Programmer's Manual* tells us that we can create objects belonging to any of these classes. We could create Leg objects, or HindLeg objects, or FrontLeg objects. In our case, we're only creating two HindLeg objects, two FrontLeg objects, and no Leg objects.

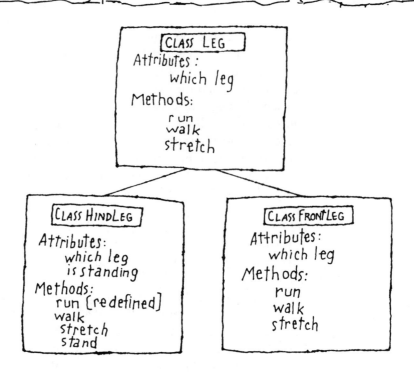

Figure 5-1 The Leg hierarchy

Bill did something else to this inheriting class business. He rewrote the Run method for the HindLeg class. The original Run method is still there inside the Leg class, and it remained the same in the FrontLeg class. But Bill rewrote (or redefined) it for the HindLeg class, to accommodate the situations where the IRD is standing on his hind legs. First, if the IRD is standing, the hind leg has to bend back down so the IRD can resume standing on all four legs, then the hind leg performs the original Run method. After all, when the Run method in the HindLeg class got redefined, the original Run method was still there, so the HindLeg can still do the original method. To try to understand things more clearly, we look back at Figure 5-1.

As we stare at the picture, things start to make more sense. Leg is the base class, and provides the main methods. But it's not specialized enough to be of any use to the real, live legs. We need to specialize it into two derived classes, HindLeg and FrontLeg. These two new classes keep a couple of the methods, change a couple, and one even adds a new method. We suppose we could also add some attributes, when we derive a new class, in the same way that HindLeg added a new method, Stand.

The Dog's Favorite Tree

As we dig through Bill's code, we find that every class is derived from another class in sort of a hierarchy, with one class at the top of the hierarchy. This one original class is called DogPiece, and every other class is somehow derived from this class. Each new class changes its base class in some way, by redefining methods, or adding new methods, or adding new attributes, or all of the above. Figure 5-2 shows some of these classes.

As each class is derived, the newly derived class becomes slightly more specialized, just like the HindLeg and FrontLeg classes made their base class, Leg, more specialized.

There won't actually be any objects of class DogPiece; rather, all objects will belong to classes derived from DogPiece. That's not to say we couldn't do it; but in our case, we need more specialization before we can create any object inside the IRD. Then what, exactly, does the DogPiece do? It contains the methods and attributes common to every class.

Up the Ladder

We see that Bill had made a note reminding him to research what happens with the constructors. *What was he talking about?* we wonder. Is there a problem with the constructors?

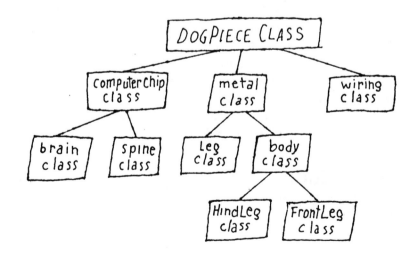

Figure 5-2 DoggyClasses

It seems that a derived class can have its own constructor, as can the class it's derived from. Bill made a note farther down the same page saying, "When an object belonging to a derived class gets created, first the parent class' constructor gets called, then the derived class' own constructor gets called. Suppose there's a three-level inheritance; that is, you have a class, then derive a class from it, and derive a third class from the second. When you create an object of the third class, first the original class' constructor gets called, then the second, then finally the third. The computer starts with the topmost class in the hierarchy and works its way down."

We look at Figure 5-2 again, and it starts to make sense. When we create a HindLeg object, first the computer does the constructor for the DogPiece class, then the constructor for the Metal class, then the constructor for the Leg class, and finally the constructor for the HindLeg class.

Don't Panic

Now we see that we can group objects by their "kind" or, preferably, "class."

We can also derive new classes from other classes:

🦴 The new classes are called derived classes.

🦴 The previous classes are called the base classes.

🦴 The process of deriving classes is called inheritance.

When we derive classes, we can add new methods or change some of the methods if necessary. This helps us keep general code in the base classes, and specific code in the derived classes.

An object can belong to any class we create, whether it's a base class or a derived class, or both.

When we create an object that's of a derived class, the base class' constructor gets called, then our derived class' constructor gets called.

Program Section

DogPiece Class

Let's try and build a couple of the classes mentioned above, using C++. We won't build all of them, but we'll build enough to make the brain class.

First, let's look again at the figure describing the hierarchy of what we'll build. It looks like Figure 5-2. Note that we'll only build a few of these classes, and that we'll want to review this table periodically as we're building the classes.

We'll start with the DogPiece class.

Recall that the DogPiece class really doesn't do much, since absolutely every piece of the dog needs to be specialized from there. So there won't be any actual objects of class DogPiece, all the actual objects will belong to classes derived from DogPiece.

Remember also that the DogPiece class contains the methods and attributes common to every class.

What, then, are the methods and attributes common to every object in the dog? Not a whole lot. But there are some.

Before we list them, remember this: When we specify that a class is to have an attribute that can be different for each object, we don't specify what the value is until we build the actual object. All we say for now is that a value goes there.

Here are some things common to each object: Each object would have a unique numeric attribute identifying the object in case it falls off and needs to be returned to the owner. This unique number can also be used for inventory purposes in general. Also, each object might need to have a size attribute, in the event that it needs replacement, since different IRDs have different sized parts.

So Listing 5-1 is the first piece of code describing the DogPiece class:

Listing 5-1 The DogPiece Class

```
#include <iostream.h>
class DogPiece
{
public:
    int SerialNumber;
    int Size;
    DogPiece(int num)
    {
        SerialNumber = num;
        cout << "Dogpiece constructor!" << endl;
    }
};
```

Go ahead and enter that into the computer. Notice that we're giving a parameter to the constructor, and this parameter is the SerialNumber. We're also printing out a message letting us know that this constructor is taking place. That'll come in handy later on, when we add more classes.

ComputerChip Class

Next we can add the ComputerChip class. The ComputerChips are each very specialized, so they really have little in common beyond the things in the DogPiece class. However, they do have in common the fact that they each process something. For instance, the eyes chip processes light images, while the mouth chip processes food. The heart chip processes blood, while the brain chip processes thoughts. So we need to give each ComputerChip a "processes" attribute.

But there's a problem. How do we do that? That is, how do we tell the computer the name of the thing it processes?

There are probably lots of ways. But we can do one thing that works quite nicely. It's called the *enum* command.

The enum command looks like this:

```
enum ProcessThings {pictures, sounds, food, thoughts, nothing };
```

This means we're creating a new type (just as int is a type) and variables of the type, ProcessThings, can take on any one of the values "pictures," "sounds," "food," "thoughts," or "nothing."

Then we can create a variable which takes on any of these values. We do it, for example, like this:

```
ProcessThings WhatItProcesses;
WhatItProcesses = sights;
```

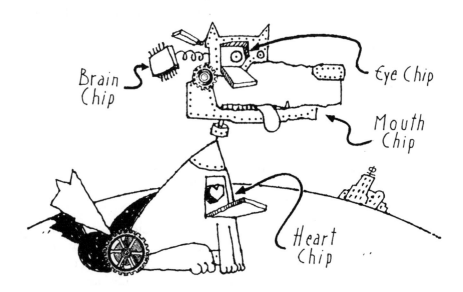

Brain Chip

Eye Chip

Mouth Chip

Heart Chip

This means the variable WhatItProcesses is of the type ProcessThings, and can take on any of the values listed above. In this case, we're giving it the value "sights."

So let's continue with the ComputerChip example, where we'll see the enum in action. Remember: ComputerChip is derived from DogPiece. The notation for deriving classes is shown in Listing 5-2, with the complete class ComputerChip.

Listing 5-2 The ComputerChip Class

```
enum ProcessThings {pictures, sounds, food, thoughts, nothing };
class ComputerChip : public DogPiece
{
public:
    ProcessThings Processes;
    ComputerChip(ProcessThings which, int num) : DogPiece(num)
    {
        Processes = which;
        cout << "ComputerChip constructor!" << endl;
    }
};
```

This means the class ComputerChip is derived or inherited from the class DogPiece, which ultimately means the object ComputerChip has not only the attribute Processes but the SerialNumber and Size attributes as well.

The word "public" before the word "DogPiece" means everything that's public in DogPiece is public in ComputerChip. (Remember, public means that it is accessible from any part of the program.) Thus SerialNumber and Size are both still public.

Notice the strange form of the constructor. The ComputerChip constructor takes two parameters, one for Processes and one for SerialNumber. We can just copy the first into the Processes attribute in the code for this constructor.

But remember that the DogPiece constructor is also going to be performed, and it needs a parameter. What parameter does it need? The SerialNumber. So when we create a ComputerChip class, where does the DogPiece constructor get its parameter? We need to pass it somehow, and that's where the strange notation

```
ComputerChip(ProcessThings which, int num) : DogPiece(num)
```

comes in. This means we pass the num parameter on to the DogPiece constructor.

Building the Brain

The next class is the Brain class. We won't make this a very thorough class; we'll only make it do a few things for now.

Objects belonging to class Brain are really made up of computer chips, so this class is derived from ComputerChip. (Note that although we only have one object of class Brain in each IRD, we still need to create a complete class.)

For now, we'll only include two methods: Remember and Forget. These methods will use an attribute that we'll call Memory. Remember will save a number in Memory, and Forget will get rid of the number, resetting Memory back to 0. Listing 5-3 shows the Brain class.

Listing 5-3 The Brain Class

```
class Brain : public ComputerChip
{
public:
    int Memory;
    Brain(int num) : ComputerChip(thoughts, num)
    {
        cout << "Brain constructor!" << endl;
    }
    void Remember(int what)
    {
        Memory = what;
    }
    void Forget()
    {
        Memory = 0;
    }
};
```

(It may help to glance again at Figure 5-2 while you follow through the next couple of sentences.) Notice that the constructor gets the serial number for a parameter, and that's passed on to the ComputerChip constructor. But the ComputerChip constructor also needs a Processes parameter, so we pass that, too. Notice we're passing an actual value, thoughts. (Remember, thoughts is a value, not a variable. It's specified in the enum statement.) We pass an actual value, because all brains process thoughts.

This concept of passing parameters up the ladder of the constructors can get pretty confusing. You might want to let it sink in a bit and then review it again later.

We can now build the main part: See Listing 5-4. We'll give a serial number of 12. Then we'll print it out, just to be sure it made it all the way up to the DogPiece class. After that, we'll print out the Processes attribute. And next we'll play a bit with the brain methods.

Listing 5-4 The Main Part

```
void main()
{
    Brain OneAndOnly(12);   // We'll make 12 the serial number.

    cout << "Serial number: " << OneAndOnly.SerialNumber;
    cout << endl << endl;

    cout << "Processes: " << OneAndOnly.Processes;
    cout << endl << endl;

    OneAndOnly.Remember(5);
    cout << "Remembering " << OneAndOnly.Memory << endl;
    OneAndOnly.Remember(10);
    cout << "Now Remembering " << OneAndOnly.Memory << endl;
    OneAndOnly.Forget();
    cout << "Now on the mind is " << OneAndOnly.Memory << endl;
}
```

The Whole Shebang

Putting it all together looks like Listing 5-5.

Listing 5-5 The Whole Shebang

```
#include <iostream.h>
class DogPiece
{
public:
    int SerialNumber;
    int Size;
    DogPiece(int num)
    {
        SerialNumber = num;
        cout << "Dogpiece constructor!" << endl;
    }
};

enum ProcessThings {pictures, sounds, food, thoughts, nothing };
class ComputerChip : public DogPiece
{
public:
    ProcessThings Processes;
    ComputerChip(ProcessThings which, int num) : DogPiece(num)
    {
        Processes = which;
        cout << "ComputerChip constructor!" << endl;
    }
};
```

continued on next page

continued from previous page

```
class Brain : public ComputerChip
{
public:
    int Memory;
    Brain(int num) : ComputerChip(thoughts, num)
    {
        cout << "Brain constructor!" << endl;
    }
    void Remember(int what)
    {
        Memory = what;
    }
    void Forget()
    {
        Memory = 0;
    }
};

void main()
{
    Brain OneAndOnly(12);    // We'll make 12 the serial number.

    cout << "Serial number: " << OneAndOnly.SerialNumber;
    cout << endl << endl;

    cout << "Processes: " << OneAndOnly.Processes;
    cout << endl << endl;

    OneAndOnly.Remember(5);
    cout << "Remembering " << OneAndOnly.Memory << endl;
    OneAndOnly.Remember(10);
    cout << "Now Remembering " << OneAndOnly.Memory << endl;
    OneAndOnly.Forget();
    cout << "Now on the mind is " << OneAndOnly.Memory << endl;
}
```

The output of this program looks like this:

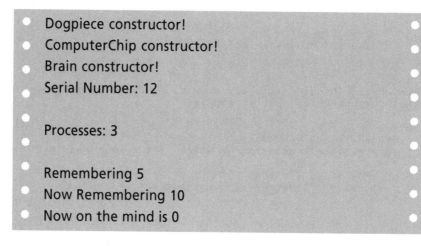

Dogpiece constructor!
ComputerChip constructor!
Brain constructor!
Serial Number: 12

Processes: 3

Remembering 5
Now Remembering 10
Now on the mind is 0

Notice the order in which our constructors are getting called.

Also notice how the parameters to the constructors are handled, and that our SerialNumber of 12 makes it all the way up to the DogPiece class. The 12 gets passed to the constructor of Brain, and then both 12 and thought get passed to the constructor of ComputerChip. ComputerChip's constructor grabs the thought and saves it, while passing the 12 on up to the DogPiece class. The DogPiece class, in turn, saves this 12 in the SerialNumber attribute.

And one more thing to look at: We're printing the value of the Processes member, but in the output it doesn't show up as the word "thought." Instead, it shows up as a number. That's a slight annoyance about C++; some other languages sometimes let you actually print the word. But C++ prints the number representing the position in the enum list, with the *first position being 0*. Because "thought" is in position 3, that's the number that shows up in the output.

A few quick points about where we're headed. When we write professional programs, generally we end up with a considerable number of classes, arranged in some gigantic hierarchy with tons of multiple inheritances, which effectively wipes out a sense of a hierarchy. As you can see here, we're already collecting quite a group of classes, and even now we're keeping the classes pretty limited. The objects in the Brain class can't yet do things like calculate or anything. Later on in Part 2, we'll expand on the classes we're building here, and we'll end up with a huge set of pretty thorough classes for an IRD.

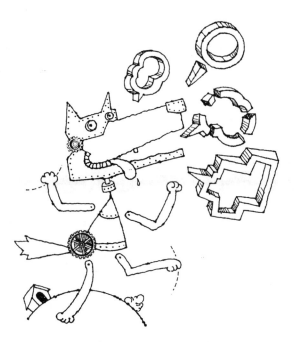

6
TERROR IN ENGINEERING: OVERLOAD!

We're putting in some extra hours at PETT late one evening, when Dr. Old shows up at our door. He comes trotting in with a smile on his face. "Hello," he says, "I thought I'd come see what you're up to."

We tell him we're trying to learn C++.

Scoping Out a Variable

"That's great," says Dr. Old. "You know, I don't really hate this new stuff as much as you may think. It's just that I think you should know a little more about the old stuff. Take methods, for instance. Most objects have methods. And these methods always do something in a step-by-step manner. Just what do they do?" He laughs. "Ha, ha, that depends on the particular method and particular class of objects! But they have at least one thing in common: When we write them, we make them perform a task. We give them a *function* to perform. We may make them process something or change something. We may make them change an attribute. Or we may make them call another method. We might even make them do all these things."

He glances out the window and continues. "The point is that these methods do their thing in a step-by-step fashion. They may loop back, but it's still step-by-step. And often, we need to give these methods a little room to work. By that I mean, when we're writing the code for a method, we may discover that the method needs to remember something."

"For instance," he continues, "suppose we have a class for an object in the IRD's brain that keeps track of the amount of money spent. This object is the Expenses object. It looks like this." Dr. Old begins writing on a conveniently located chalkboard:

OBJECT: Expenses

He says, "The MonthlyGrocery attribute is where we keep the total for the amount of groceries the IRD bought this month. When the IRD goes on a grocery shopping trip, he needs to keep a running total of how much he's spending; and when he's done shopping, he adds this total to his MonthlyGrocery attribute. He really doesn't keep a record of how much money he's spent on each grocery trip; he's not that sophisticated yet. All he cares is how much money he's spent by the end of the month. So the running total for the shopping trip is just temporary, and after the shopping trip is done and the running total's been added into the MonthlyGrocery attribute, the running total goes away into oblivion." He waves his hands in the air.

"So," he says, "let's make a method here for the Expenses object. This method is called GroceryTrip, and it's the one that adds up the grocery bill for a single shopping trip and adds this total to the final MonthlyGrocery attribute within the Expenses object. So what's the procedure? What's the step-by-step approach to this method? Remember, once we've got the object broken down to its methods, we can program the method in a step-by-step approach. So what are the steps?"

We point out that we need to add up the items being bought for this grocery trip, and add that amount to the MonthlyGrocery attribute.

"So how do you do that?" he asks.

We're not sure what he means.

"How do you add up the items? For instance, if you're doing it manually, with the help of a calculator, what would you do?"

"Well, we'd type in the first amount, hit the add key, type in the second, hit the add key again, type in the third, on and on, until we've covered all the items."

"Exactly. So let's do the same thing. But we need to be a little more precise in how we tell the computer how to do that. The calculator serves what purpose?"

"To add the numbers."

"But what else?" asks Dr. Old.

"What do you mean, what else?"

"I mean the calculator doesn't just add two numbers. If that were all, we'd have to add the first two, and remember the answer. Then we'd type in the answer and add the third number, getting a new answer. But that's not what happens, right?"

"Right, it keeps track of the answer."

"It keeps a running total," says Dr. Old.

"Yup."

"So we need to tell the computer to keep a running total. And this is the temporary variable I mentioned earlier on. We need to tell the computer to *create* a temporary variable representing the running total. Then what do we do?" he asks.

"We add the first two and put the answer in this running total."

"Then after that happens, what do we do?"

"We add the third item on to the running total, then the fourth, then the fifth, until we're through."

"So we've got two distinct steps. The first process adds the first two and puts the answer in our running total. The second process loops through the remaining items, adding each amount to this total. Is there a better way to do it? Can we come up with a process that's the same for all items, rather than have something special for the first two items?"

"Well . . ." We think for a moment.

Dr. Old continues, "Imagine the running total as a tank, and one by one we'll add the amounts into this tank. What's the initial amount in the tank, before we put anything in it?"

"It's empty, so it would be zero."

"Right. Then we add the first item into it, and what happens?"

"It gets the value of the first item."

"Why?"

We laugh. "Because zero plus any number is that same number."

"Of course! So then we add in the second item. Same process, right?"

"Sure."

"Then the third item. And the fourth and fifth. And so on for each item."

"Okay."

"So let's express that as a set of steps." Dr. Old approaches the chalk-board. "We need to initialize the running total, as we just said. What's its initial amount?"

"Zero."

"Exactly." He writes:

```
Object: Expenses
Method: GroceryTrip
RunningTotal is an integer
RunningTotal = 0
```

He continues, "I wrote the third line because we have to tell the com-puter about this temporary storage space it's supposed to make. Remember that these temporary variables are like lines on a sheet of notebook paper, and we have to tell the computer to make a new line, and we have to give that line a name, along with a type. This type is integer. Okay! Next, we need to begin adding each item in one by one. Which construct do we use?"

"Construct? Oh yeah, Linda used that term yesterday. Now what does that mean again . . . ?"

"Which form of a loop do we use? Do-while, while, for . . . ?"

"Well, we could use any form, I suppose."

"Let's use the while construct, then. What's the condition? While what is true do we do the process of adding items?"

"While there are items left."

"Perfect!" He writes more on the chalkboard, so it looks like this:

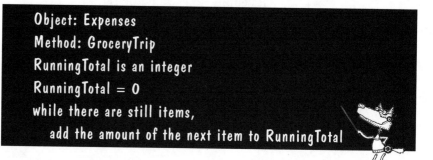

```
Object: Expenses
Method: GroceryTrip
RunningTotal is an integer
RunningTotal = 0
while there are still items,
    add the amount of the next item to RunningTotal
```

"Then, what was the original problem? Can't forget that, hmmm?"

"We had to add this running total to the MonthlyGrocery attribute."

"Yup!" He writes:

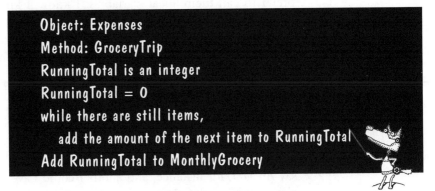

```
Object: Expenses
Method: GroceryTrip
RunningTotal is an integer

RunningTotal = 0
while there are still items,
        add the amount of the next item to RunningTotal
Add RunningTotal to MonthlyGrocery
```

"And that's it!" He smiles and looks around the room, as if he's expecting a crowd to applaud.

We're starting to like this man, too. He has a great way of explaining things.

"Now," he continues, "this RunningTotal is simply a temporary variable, as we talked about above. And what happens to the temporary variable when the computer finishes executing this method?"

"Well, we no longer need it."

"That's right. So it gets rid of it. In fact, it has to get rid of it by the rules of programming. We could probably build a computer that doesn't get rid of its temporary variables, but it would be very messy, and probably wouldn't work right all the time. So we build our computers to get rid of their temporary variables at the end of the methods in which they're created. We say the temporary variable has a scope consisting of the method it's created in."

"Scope?"

"Yeah. The *scope* is the space during which the variable is in existence. It's in existence during the execution of this method, so the scope of this variable is this method."

"I see. I'll try and remember that word, but I can't guarantee I will."

He grins. "No problem! Learning to program ain't easy!"

A Variable of the Same Name

Dr. Old stares quietly out the window for a while, collecting his thoughts, when he finally speaks again. "There's one more thing you should know. The word 'temporary' is acceptable, but those darn computer scientists who like to confuse the world had to go and use a different word. They prefer to call them 'local' variables. I know, I know, it's annoying, but it's a fact of life. I prefer the word 'temporary,' but nobody would know what I was talking about if I used that word—which is a little ironic, considering that's the word I used to teach you about them! Hahaha! But we'll use the word 'local' from now on."

"I might point out," he adds, "that it's also perfectly acceptable for a method to have more than one local variable. In fact, many have lots and lots!" He looks at the ceiling. "Lots and lots."

He looks back at us and continues, "Now, back to the methods. We could have two different methods, and one could have a local variable, say *Amount*, for instance, and another could have its own local variable, also called *Amount*. They are separate local variables, each within their own methods, and they have nothing to do with each other. This is perfectly acceptable and quite common, in fact. Two methods may have their local variables named the same, but they are still completely separate, because the scope of each local variable is still the method it's inside."

"But," he continues, "be sure and use names that make sense for your temporary—er, local—variables. A good name for the example above is *RunningTotal*. We could have used something like *a* or *x500* or whatever, but those don't make sense for the problem at hand. It's best to use names that make sense, names that describe what the variable is used for."

Dr. Old glances at his watch. "Oh, my goodness, I almost forgot. I have an appointment in an hour. Me and the boys got a gig."

"A gig?"

"Sure, you know, a performance. I play keyboards in a rock band." He hurries out the door.

After he leaves, we review what he talked about. It looks like when we design methods, we write them in a step-by-step fashion, and we're free to create some temporary local variables to store things. But these local variables are temporary, and they go away after the method is done, so we have to use them wisely. In the example above, we added the value of the local variable *RunningTotal* to the attribute MonthlyGrocery.

A Method of the Same Name

We then think about some stuff Dr. Old said earlier on. He said that each method must perform a specific function. Well, that makes sense. But the other day he talked about how we can write methods to give us back something if we wish. They can give us back a number, or pretty much anything. Interesting.

The door flies open. It's Dr. Old again. "Sorry, I got halfway there and remembered a couple of things I forgot to say. I could have used the IRD to communicate, but I left mine in my office. Anyway, here's the POOP scoop: Remember the other day, we were talking . . . ."

"About methods returning things?" we ask.

"Um, yeah, um . . . Anyway, these methods can return something if we want them to, but they don't have to. And, of course, they can take things as parameters. And these parameters are each of a certain type, right?"

"Sure."

"Well, believe it or not, our C++ compilers are pretty smart, and we can have within a *single class of objects* two methods that have the same name, as long as they take a different set of parameters. Does that make sense? Probably not. Let's look at an example."

He approaches the chalkboard and says, "Let's say you want to have two methods for grocery shopping. One figures sales tax at the end for when the IRD is visiting one of those annoying states that require sales tax on food. And the other one is like the one we created above that doesn't do anything with sales tax. Well, we can make two methods, one that takes as a parameter a sales tax rate. The other one takes no parameters. Here are the two methods:"

```
GroceryTrip(salestax)
GroceryTrip()
```

"There!" He stomps his foot. "That should do it! Yes, yes, very nice, very nice. We have two functions within one class of objects, and these functions have the same name! The C++ compiler doesn't mind, either, because it can figure out which method we're activating by looking at the number and types of parameters we're passing. In this case, we're either passing one parameter, a number representing sales tax, or no parameter at all. If we pass a single number, it must be the first method we're using. If we pass no parameters, it's the second method. If we try to pass any other combination of parameters, we'll get an error. The compiler will halt and give us some sort of error message telling us we have to correct the mistake."

We think about that. It seems to make sense! More than one method with the same name. "But why would we do that?" we ask. "That could get confusing for us, the programmers!"

"Ah, but not really. We can use the GroceryTrip method in other parts of our program, and we don't need to worry so much about the parameters. We can write code that passes sales tax as a parameter, or we could write code that doesn't pass any parameters. The hope is that the methods will be able to handle any situation that arises. In this case, there are basically two situations: one case where there is a sales tax, the other case where there is no sales tax. By the way, we call this *overloading*. We're overloading the first method we created."

Every Method Performs a Function

"There was something else," says Dr. Old, "that you were thinking about while I was gone. You were thinking about how I was saying each method must perform a function. Well, I thought I'd add that for that reason, we sometimes refer to methods as functions. Sure, it gets confusing. But there's another reason. In the old days, before object-oriented programming, we didn't have objects, yet we needed things that were similar to methods. So what we had were programs each with a whole big group of methods, and we called these methods functions. We hadn't even come up with the word method yet.

"Worse, we also had a big batch of attributes that were for the whole program, and these methods could directly access these attributes. These particular attributes were called global variables.

"These functions that we wrote were stand-alone functions that behaved similarly to methods, only they operated these global variables. If it sounds messy and confusing, it is. But, there are times, actually, where we still want to write stand-alone functions in C++. Now, I warn you, there are people out there who are real OOP advocates who would probably scoff at the idea. But C++ lets us do it, so we may as well know *how* to do it.

"Let's look at an example. Maybe that will help clear up this mess I've created." He erases the chalkboard. "One mess gone. Now let's clear up the second one. Let's see. Suppose you have a local variable that represents the number of apples the IRD has in his pocket. And suppose we want to find out what that number times itself is—that is, we want to find out what the square of the number is. One approach we can

Figure 6-1 Square function

take is to write a stand-alone function that does the hard part of squaring the number. Then, any time we want to square a number, we just call this function." He writes Figure 6-1 on the chalkboard.

"There!" says Dr. Old. "That's good. Very nice drawing, hmmm? And remember, this is a stand-alone function. We may need to write this function ourselves, and if it's done properly, every method in our entire program can use this function. It really comes in handy. Of course, there are probably ways we could solve this problem in OOP, but I don't really care about that right now. This is a feature in C++, and lots of people use it, so we can use it on occasion, too. Sound good?"

"Sure!" We always like to break the rules.

Don't Panic

Here's what we've seen today:

- local variables
- functions

    overloading methods

    letting methods use the same local variable names

Program Section

Local Variables

We've already seen some examples of local variables in Chapter 2. The examples in the section called Variables was really a demonstration of local variables whose scope was the main function. But let's look at a couple more, emphasizing the scope—that is, where the variables can and cannot be used.

Notice the part of the Listing 6-1 beginning with

```
void Expenses :: GroceryTrip()
```

This is the code for the GroceryTrip method. In previous chapters we had the code inside the class definition. That works, but it can get messy if the code for your method is longer than a line or two. So C++ has an alternative: Only put a line in the class definition stating that the method is there, what parameters it takes, and what it returns. Then, later on, outside the class definition, have the code for the method. (Sometimes this is called the function body.) This is the way we're doing it here. Notice the format for the code part. The type of thing being returned goes first (in this case, nothing is returned, so it's void). Next is the class name. Two colons follow. Then comes the name of the method and its parameter list. The actual code, as before, is inside curly brackets. The whole class is in Listing 6-1.

Listing 6-1 The GroceryTrip Method

```
#include <iostream.h>

class Expenses
{
private:
    int MonthlyGrocery;
public:
    Expenses()  //constructor.  Initialize MonthlyGrocery
        { MonthlyGrocery = 0; }
    void GroceryTrip();
    int Total()
        { return MonthlyGrocery; }
};
```

```
void Expenses :: GroceryTrip()
{
    int RunningTotal;
    int NextAmount;
    int i;

    RunningTotal = 0;
    for (i=0; i<5; i++)
    {
        cout << "Enter the next amount." << endl;
        cin >> NextAmount;
        RunningTotal += NextAmount;
    }
    MonthlyGrocery += RunningTotal;
}


void main()
{
    Expenses ThisMonth;
    cout << "Doing first grocery trip..." << endl;
    ThisMonth.GroceryTrip();
    cout << "Total so far: " << ThisMonth.Total() << endl;
    cout << "Doing second grocery trip..." << endl;
    ThisMonth.GroceryTrip();
    cout << "Total so far: " << ThisMonth.Total() << endl;
}
```

The output of this program is

```
Doing first grocery trip...
Enter the next amount.
3
Enter the next amount.
4
Enter the next amount.
2
Enter the next amount.
10
Enter the next amount.
15
Total so far: 34
```

continued on next page

continued from previous page

```
Doing second grocery trip...
Enter the next amount.
8
Enter the next amount.
6
Enter the next amount.
10
Enter the next amount.
7
Enter the next amount.
11
Total so far: 76
```

You might try putting in some sort of reference in main to one of GroceryTrip's local variables. For instance, you might put this in main:

```
cout << RunningTotal;
```

and try to compile it. You should get an error, since *RunningTotal* is being referred to outside its scope.

Overloading

Listing 6-2 demonstrates function overloading. Notice the HungryDog class has two methods called Eat. That's fine, as long as they have different parameters, which they do. One has no parameters; the other has one integer for a parameter. (The type and number of parameters is the way the compiler can distinguish the two when we use them later on.)

Listing 6-2 Function Overloading

```
#include <iostream.h>

class HungryDog {
private:
    int Food;
public:
    HungryDog()
    {    Food = 0;      }
    void Eat()
```

```
    {     Food += 10;        }
    void Eat(int Amount)
    {     Food += Amount; }
    int GetFood()
    {     return Food;      }
};

void main()
{
    HungryDog big;
    cout << "Food = " << big.GetFood() << endl;
    big.Eat(5);
    cout << "Just ate 5 for total of ";
    cout << big.GetFood() << endl;

    big.Eat();
    cout << "Just ate the standard amount for total of ";
    cout << big.GetFood() << endl;
}
```

Notice that in the main we're calling both forms of Eat. First, we're calling the second form, which takes a single integer for a parameter. Then we're calling the first form, which takes no parameters.

The output of this program looks like this:

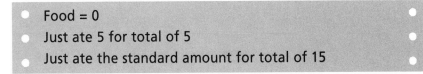

```
Food = 0
Just ate 5 for total of 5
Just ate the standard amount for total of 15
```

Stand-alone Functions

Listing 6-3 is an example from a popular child-IRD TV show, and has an example of a stand-alone function. Some OOP advocates might not like having a stand-alone function in a C++ program, but the fact is that C++ supports them (because they were part of its parent language, C) and so we should probably know how to use them.

Listing 6-3 Big IRD

```
#include <iostream.h>

int Square(int number)
{
    return number * number;
}
```

continued on next page

continued from previous page

```
void main ()
{
    int apples;

    apples = 3;
    cout << "Big IRD has " << apples << " apples.";

    cout << " If we square them, we get ";
    cout << Square(apples) << endl;
}
```

Notice when we call the square function, we don't specify an object, since it doesn't have one; we just give the function name.

The output of this program is

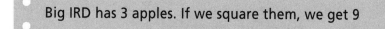

Big IRD has 3 apples. If we square them, we get 9

7

WEARING THE DOG'S GLASSES: SEEING OBJECTS

As we look out into the courtyard from the cafeteria, we can see the IRDs running around in the Doggytrainer facilities. This training program helps the IRDs to perfect their skills, such as running, eating, and guarding property.

We remember when our personal IRD had to go through the training, and how proud we were of him. It hardly seems like it was that long ago that we saw the engineers piecing him together, object by object, and then taking him out to the Doggytrainer. Yet, it's been a whole two weeks.

Interfacing to the IRD's Objects

We fondly think back to the day they were putting him together. Bill was on hand, explaining each piece. Most of the internal stuff was just electronic parts, but the external stuff made our IRD look like a dog.

Bill explained that each real-world part—the legs, the head, and so on—is what's known as the *interface object*. The objects inside the computer memory are the *simulated memory object*.

To make his point clear, Bill gave us an analogy that actually made sense. He said that we humans use the brain to process information for our arms and legs and other parts. Deep inside our heads, the brain keeps track of where the arms are and what they are doing. This is the simulated

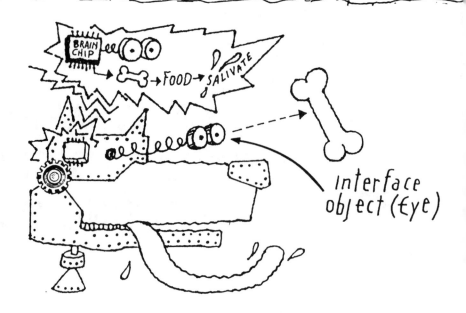

memory object. Then, when the thinking part of the brain decides we should lift our arm, that part of the brain tells the part of the brain controlling the arm to lift its interface object, the actual arm. That part of the brain, in turn, sends a nerve message to the arm to be lifted.

So the arm is represented by two things. The arm that we see—the thing holding onto the chocolate milkshake—is the interface unit, the first part. The part of the brain that controls the arm—the simulated memory object—is the second part.

The same is true for the IRD. One part of the IRD's brain controls, say, his left hind leg. This simulated memory object inside the brain has all the details for the object—that is, it has the attributes and methods. The physical leg is the interface unit that does the actual moving.

Here's another example: the IRD's eye. This object is simulated inside the brain by the computer program, and this simulated object contains the methods and attributes. The eyeball itself is the interface object. This interface object receives pictures from the outside world and these pictures are what the simulated object processes in its methods.

Often when Bill referred to the Eye object, he was referring to the simulated one inside the IRD's brain. Since Bill's gone, we should probably continue that practice in his honor. Of course, we don't *have* to. But we should.

As for the actual eyeball, Bill refers to that as the interface unit. So he has the Eye object, and its interface unit. Check out Figure 7-1 for an audio/visual aid. (You'll have to imagine the audio part.)

Figure 7-2 has the same type of picture for the Leg object. Notice the HindLeg object's interface unit does only movement, while the Eye object's interface unit receives input. It's like a one-way street. The HindLeg's interface unit responds to commands from the brain, while the eye's interface unit sends messages back to the brain. Yet both are interface units.

Bill had also explained that often objects don't have interface units. But when they do, they cannot share interface units. Each interface unit connects to only one object.

No Interface

As we continue watching the courtyard, we think about some of the stuff Bill told us. He said that some objects have no interface unit. So what good are those objects? Why should an object not have a connection to

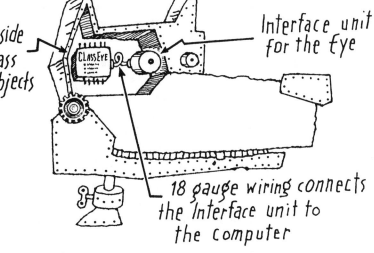

Figure 7-1 Audio/visual aid for the Eye object. For the audio part, imagine the "1812 Overture"

computer inside
holds the
Hind Leg class
and its two
objects

Two interface units,
one for each
object
of class
Hind Leg

Figure 7-2 Audio/visual aid for the HindLeg objects. For the audio part,
imagine the "Minute Waltz"

the real world? Aren't objects supposed to model or simulate the real-world things?

We would have asked Bill at the time, but frankly, we were only half-listening. After all, Bill's not exactly a top-notch conversationalist.

So what would be an example of an object that doesn't have an interface unit? We remember seeing in Bill's program an object of class VitalInfo that contained the Name, Address, and Owner attributes. The Name attribute is a short, single-word name that we can call the IRD by. The Address is where the IRD lives. The Owner is our name.

Should this have an interface unit? We can't really think of an interface unit for it, so apparently this is an example of an object with no interface unit.

We grab our handy-dandy *IRD Programmer's Manual* and see what it says. Surprise! There's an example. But it's not a very good one. So instead we grab the *Example Book for Simple C++*. Since *Example Book* only exists in the author's mind, we politely ask the author to show us the examples. He agrees, and they're presented here.

Objects with Interface Units

We've already seen some objects with interface units: the eyes and the hind legs. Here are some more examples:

- The mouth
- The ears
- The door in the computerized IRDMobile. That's the door that, if not shut all the way, causes the IRDMobile to not run, and the IRDMobile calls the door a jar.

Objects with No Interface Units

Bill had explained that it's important to realize objects exist that don't have interface objects. After all, he liked to argue that everything is an object. We sometimes agreed, depending on how philosophical we were feeling at the time.

But regardless, here are some examples of objects without interface units:

- The VitalInfo object holding the Name, Address, and Owner information.
- The EnergyLevel object
- The Budget object

We could actually argue that the EnergyLevel object has an interface unit, the actual energy, and that the Budget objects have interface units, the money. But we won't argue.

Don't Panic

So we see that objects simulate things in the real world, whether or not they are concrete things that we can touch. Sometimes objects have interface units attached to them, to provide a link between the object and the real world. But sometimes they don't.

Program Section

We tell the author to take a breather and leave out the Program Section. Besides, we've already glanced ahead and noticed that Chapter 9 is sort of a continuation of this chapter. We mention that to the author, and quickly put down *Simple C++* before we have a chance to see if the author is listening.

8
POINTERS
& OTHER
BREEDS OF DOGS

Another weekend is finally here, and we're out early Saturday morning walking our IRD. The IRD is glancing at each house we pass, and we wonder if perhaps he's memorizing the names and addresses on the mailboxes. We quietly think to ourselves, "That list could come in handy for a salesman. It would be a directory of all the people's names in order of address!"

That's when it hits us what the *IRD Programmer's Manual* was trying fruitlessly to tell us: Variables are a lot like houses. If we have a street filled with houses, and by some chance each house holds a family with a different name, we can specify any house on the street just by the name of the family.

So it is with variables: Within a given scope, we can access any variable simply by its name. We remember that variables are a lot like lines on a sheet of notebook paper, and each has a name.

But the houses have addresses, and we can use these addresses to specify the houses, too. And again, so it is with variables. If we wanted to, we could number each line on the notebook paper inside the computer's memory. Then each variable could be accessed by these numbers (or "addresses") rather than by the names of the variables.

In short, each house on this particular street has both a unique name (the owner's family name) and a unique address. Likewise, variables have both a name that's unique within their scope, as well as an address that's always unique.

Figure 8-1 The big house takes up two addresses, but only the first is used

More Room for a Bigger House

As we're walking our IRD, we stumble across an extra-large, economy-size house sprawling across two lots. We're looking at the addresses, and we realize each lot gets an address. Since this house takes up two lots, it also takes up two addresses. But the builder only put one of the two addresses on the house. Figure 8-1 demonstrates this.

There's another similarity to computers: The house that takes up two lots and two addresses is just like some variables inside the computer. Indeed, some variables store more information, and therefore take up more room inside the computer memory. This means they take up more than one address.

This is amazing! This particular street is so analogous to computers that it's almost as if we're living inside a world completely contrived for the sake of example! We quietly ponder this for a moment, while our IRD looks around for a fire hydrant.

The Pointer's House

As we venture farther down the road, we come across a house whose owners are clearly on vacation. How do we know that? Because their burglar-guard timer must be messed up: We can see that the lamp in the front room is on, yet it's daylight out. It probably shuts off at night. There's also a note on the mailbox for everyone to see. It says:

> *Dear Mailcarrier:*
>
> *Please leave all mail for me at my neighbor's house,*
>
> *address 112.*
>
> *Thanks,*
>
> *Bill, address 114*

So we think about the situation: Bill lives in house 114, and his mail is sitting inside house 112. If we want to find out information about Bill, we can take two approaches. First, we can go directly into his house, which is house 114. Or, we can get the information indirectly by going into house 112 and reading Bill's mail.

We remember reading about such situations in the *IRD Programmer's Manual*. Apparently, such a house as 112 would be a *pointer*. It has an address (112), but *contains* another address (114). That is, it points to 114. Well, maybe not—point is another computer term that only makes partial sense. But most programmers use it, so we should probably use it so they know what we're talking about.

We approach house 112, which is holding Bill's mail. We knock, and a grumpy old man answers the door.

"What!" he snaps.

We ask if he's holding Bill's mail.

"I sure am. And I'm sick of it. It seems the neighborhood has deemed me the local mail holder. Last week I held the mail for that guy in 108. This week it's that fool in 114. But I've laid down the law: At any single moment, I will only hold mail for one house. Never more than that. Gets too confusing! So after Bill's back, I'll give him his mail, and only then can I hold your mail!" He slams the door in our face.

The *IRD Programmer's Manual* had a similar description when we looked through it yesterday. Only it was for computers, not houses.

It seems a variable can also be deemed a pointer, and it can hold the address of another variable. It can only hold one address at a time, and we can change the variables whose address it holds.

We head back to our own house to see if Bill's notes have an example. We happened to bring his notes home, just in case we needed them.

Back Home

We arrive home and look through Bill's notebook. Of course, there's an appropriate example.

Bill writes,

> *Alas, I have stumbled upon a problem. Nevertheless, my superior intellect has prevailed, and I have solved the problem! The problem was this: I need to pass a large object as a parameter to a function, and it's causing all sorts of problems. The solution? Pass a pointer to the object instead. Why? Because a pointer takes up less space than an entire object. Thus, it's easier to pass!*

Well, that seems pretty stupid. Pass a pointer instead of an object. Because then the function taking the parameter has to go through the trouble of accessing the object indirectly through the pointer.

Of course, Bill did say it's easier to pass a pointer, so maybe that's the reason for doing it.

Bill had written more about it:

> *Oh, ye reader, there's more to it than that.*

Egads, he's a terrible writer!

> *Really, kind reader, in the old C language, you were required to pass pointers as parameters to functions. You*

> *weren't allowed to pass anything much more complicated than that, except for simple little variables. And C++ has included this concept, even though there are other ways around it.*

Gosh, that's getting pretty confusing. Let's not sweat over it just yet; we'll leave the rest for the Program Section, when we can see some real-live examples.

Don't Panic

As usual, we won't panic. If we didn't quite understand absolutely every concept here, we just won't worry about it! C++ can wait!

Here are the topics we've seen:

- addresses
- pointers

And not a whole lot more! So let's call it a day. (Unless we're ambitious and ready to dive right into the Program Section!)

Program Section

We don't have a computer at home, so we drive back to the office. That's reason enough to skip the Program Section, but we decide we need to learn this C++ stuff for the sake of job security.

Back at work, we look at some examples.

Example 1: Pointers to Integers

This example demonstrates the proper format for using pointer variables. The * means the variable is a pointer, and the & means "address of." For example,

```
int *Pointer;
```

means *Pointer* is a pointer to an integer. That is, it holds the address of an integer variable. Which integer variable? Doesn't matter. It can be any integer variable. We'll make it hold the address of the integer called PointedTo. The way we do that is to put:

```
Pointer = &PointedTo;
```

And *Pointer* now holds the address of &PointedTo. Check out this whole example now in Listing 8-1.

Listing 8-1 Pointers 1

```
#include <fstream.h>

void main()
{
    int PointedTo;
    int *Pointer;

    PointedTo = 5;
    Pointer = &PointedTo;  // Pointer gets the
                           // address of PointedTo.

    cout << "PointedTo = " << PointedTo << endl;
    cout << "Pointer points to a variable holding ";
    cout << *Pointer << endl;

    *Pointer = 6;

    cout << "PointedTo = " << PointedTo << endl;
    cout << "Pointer points to a variable holding ";
    cout << *Pointer << endl;
}
```

Notice the line:

```
*Pointer = 6;
```

This means "the thing Pointer points to is to be set to 6." In this case, since *Pointer* points to PointedTo, PointedTo becomes 6.

The output for this program looks like this:

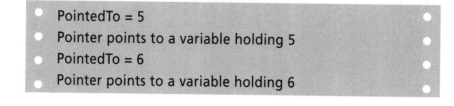

```
PointedTo = 5
Pointer points to a variable holding 5
PointedTo = 6
Pointer points to a variable holding 6
```

Example 2: More Pointers to Integers

We can make the example a little more sophisticated by adding another variable. Carefully look through this example (Listing 8-2).

Listing 8-2 Pointers 2

```
#include <iostream.h>

void main()
{
    int PointedTo, Another, *Pointer;

    PointedTo = 5;
    Another   = 10;

    Pointer = &PointedTo;  // Pointer gets the
                           // address of PointedTo.

    cout << "PointedTo = " << PointedTo << endl;
    cout << "Pointer points to a variable holding ";
    cout << *Pointer << endl;

    Pointer = &Another;

    cout << "Another = " << Another << endl;
    cout << "Pointer now points to a variable holding ";
    cout << *Pointer << endl;
}
```

First, notice how we combined the variables onto one line when we declared them. This may or may not be good (it could be difficult for us humans to read), but it is rather common. This line means that PointedTo and Another are both integers, and *Pointer* is a pointer to an integer.

The output for this program should be

PointedTo = 5
Pointer points to a variable holding 5
Another = 10
Pointer now points to a variable holding 10

Example 3: Pointers to Objects

We can also make something a pointer to an object. For that matter, we can make pointers to nearly anything. Listing 8-3 shows an object and a pointer to it.

Listing 8-3 Pointers 3

```cpp
#include <iostream.h>

class Dog
{
public:
    int bark;
};

void main()
{
    Dog FirstDog;
    Dog *MyDog;

    FirstDog.bark = 5;

    cout << "Firstdog.bark = " << FirstDog.bark << endl;

    MyDog = &FirstDog;

    cout << "MyDog is a pointer and points to FirstDog." << endl;
    cout << "To prove it, *MyDog has a bark level of ";
    cout << (*MyDog).bark << endl;
}
```

In this example MyDog is a pointer and points to FirstDog. We then output the bark level to verify that it works.

Notice the parentheses in

```cpp
(*MyDog).bark
```

This is simply to avoid ambiguity. In general, C++ lets us use lots and lots of parentheses in order to avoid ambiguity. If we had left out the parentheses and had just

```cpp
*MyDog.bark
```

we could interpret it in at least two ways, and so could the computer. First, we might say this means "The thing MyDog.bark points to." But really, we mean, "The bark level of the thing MyDog points to." So to clarify it, we add the parentheses to tell C++ to *first* find the thing MyDog points to. (It first evaluates what's in parentheses.) Next, take the bark level.

When you run this program you should see

> Firstdog.bark = 5
>
> MyDog is a pointer and points to FirstDog.
>
> To prove it, *MyDog has a bark level of 5

Example 4: A Shortcut

In the previous example, we used the strange notation

```
(*MyDog).bark
```

to access the bark attribute of the thing MyDog is pointing to. In C++ (and in C), this is so common that the inventors of the original C language gave us a shorthand notation. The above statement could be written

```
MyDog->bark
```

to get the same results. (That's a minus sign followed by a greater-than sign.) This means "the bark member of the object which MyDog points to." We can do this anytime we want or need, as long as the pointer variable points to the right class. That is, in this case, MyDog has to be a pointer to an object that has a bark attribute. Otherwise, the compiler will give us an error.

Another very common error is to put a period between the pointer variable and the attribute, rather than the ->.

So Listing 8-4 is the previous example rewritten ever-so-slightly to use this new notation. There's also an added method to show that you can use the same notation for accessing methods of objects that we're pointing something to.

Listing 8-4 Pointers 4

```
#include <iostream.h>

class Dog
{
public:
    int bark;
    void ResetBark()
    {
        bark = 0;
    }
};

void main()
{
    Dog FirstDog;
    Dog *MyDog;

    FirstDog.bark = 5;

    cout << "Firstdog.bar = " << FirstDog.bark << endl;

    MyDog = &FirstDog;
```

continued on next page

continued from previous page

```
    cout << "MyDog is a pointer and points to FirstDog." << endl;
    cout << "To prove it, *MyDog has a bark level of ";
    cout << MyDog->bark << endl;

    cout << "Now let's reset the bark level..." << endl;
    MyDog->ResetBark();
    cout << "Bark level has been reset to ";
    cout << MyDog->bark << endl;
}
```

Running this program generates

> Firstdog.bar = 5
>
> MyDog is a pointer and points to FirstDog.
>
> To prove it, *MyDog has a bark level of 5
>
> Now let's reset the bark level...
>
> Bark level has been reset to 0

Example 5: Waiting to Initialize

Pointers to objects are handy, because we can wait to initialize the object. This is handy, because sometimes we might not have the initialization data until later on. Listing 8-5 is an example:

Listing 8-5 Pointers 5

```
#include <iostream.h>

class Dog
{
public:
    int bark;
    Dog(int level)
    {
        cout << "...constructing..." << endl;
        bark = level;
    }
};

void main()
{
    Dog *Patience;
    int start;

    cout << "Enter number to initialize dog with! " << endl;
    cin >> start;
```

```
cout << "Gearing up to initialize!  Patience!" << endl;
cout << "waiting... waiting... waiting..." << endl;

Patience = new Dog(start);

cout << "We did it!  Bark level is ";
cout << Patience->bark << endl;

delete Patience;
}
```

The new thing in this program is called the *new operator*. Its job is to do just that: Make a new object. It returns a pointer to the object it just created. So in this case, the line

```
Patience = new Dog(5);
```

instructs the computer to "make a new ConstructorDog object with the value of 5 passed to the constructor. Give me back the address of the newly created object, and we'll save that address in the Patience variable."

When we use new, we have to undo our work at the end of the function with the delete operator. (Really, the computer will often clean up for us, but not always. Generally, it's a good idea to use the delete operator.)

When you run this program, the output should look like this:

```
Enter number to initialize dog with!
5
Gearing up to initialize! Patience!
waiting... waiting... waiting...
...constructing...
We did it! Bark level is 5
```

Example 6: Destruction!

In the previous example, we gave a class a method called the Constructor. Recall that this method gets called each time we create a new object belonging to this class. The reason for having a Constructor is for initialization.

As it turns out, you can also specify in C++ a method to get called when an object gets gotten rid of. This method is called a Destructor.

Remember, the constructor always gets the same name as the class. The destructor also gets this name, but is preceded by a tilde (~) symbol.

Listing 8-6 is an example of a class containing a Destructor. The Destructor function gets called each time an object of this class is deleted.

Listing 8-6 Pointers 6

```
#include <iostream.h>

class Dog
{
public:
    int bark;
    Dog(int level)
    {
        cout << "...constructing..." << endl;
        bark = level;
    }

    ~Dog()
    { cout << "Destruction!!!!" << endl; }
};

void main()
{
    Dog *Patience;
    int start;

    cout << "Enter number to initialize dog with! " << endl;
    cin >> start;

    cout << "Gearing up to initialize!  Patience!" << endl;
    cout << "waiting... waiting... waiting..." << endl;

    Patience = new Dog(start);

    cout << "We did it!  Bark level is ";
    cout << Patience->bark << endl;
    cout << "Now let's destruct..." << endl;

    delete Patience;
}
```

Here's the output:

```
Enter number to initialize dog with!
5
Gearing up to initialize! Patience!
waiting... waiting... waiting...
```

```
...constructing...
We did it! Bark level is 5
Now let's destruct...
Destruction!!!!
```

We could explore some other things in the world of pointers, but we'll hold off. That's probably enough examples for now. There are more examples in Sample Programs later in this book.

9

WELCOME TO
THE BREED:
BUILDING CLASSES

It's Saturday afternoon, and we're a little bored. We've finished walking our IRD, and we're just sitting here doing nothing. We could do something like wash the car or whatever, or we could just lounge around.

Lounging around sounds pretty good.

There's a knock at the door. We climb off the couch and go see who it is. We look out the little peek-hole. Oh, yeah. Someone from TFP, Toys for Pets, was coming over this afternoon to install a new computer in our IRDHouse out back.

We open the door and he comes in.

Installing a New Computer

"Howdy," the TFP guy says. He has a high, nasally voice. "Came to install this here computer jobbie. Gotta go in your IRDHouse. Supposed to add some automation features. If you know how to program it, that is."

"No problem," we say confidently. "I'm a programmer!"

"Great! Well, let's hop on back and install it. Er, I assume the IRDHouse is out back."

We nod. He heads around to the back of the house, and we cut through the kitchen and head outside to meet him.

We approach the IRDHouse. We knock on the door, and there's no answer. Then we see why. The IRD is sitting by the swimming pool behind his house. No problem, we'll go inside anyway.

We enter the front room. There's a couch and an entertainment center there. We notice our favorite compact disc has managed to find its way into the IRD's CD player. So that's where it went.

We head through the living room, past the kitchen, and enter the indoor fitness center.

Finally, we arrive at our destination: the racquetball courts. We were a little jealous when the IRD wanted them included in his house, but we figured he's the one with a million-dollar budget, not us.

The TFP guy opens the little door to the first racquetball court. "I assume it's this one that needs the computer," he says.

We have no idea, so we just nod.

He reaches behind the door and snaps the computer in place. "There," he says. "Done." He grins and stands there. We're not sure what he wants now. He holds out his hand, palm up. We shake it. "Thanks!" we say. He frowns. We let go of his hand and he's still holding it out. "What?" we say.

"Nothing." he snaps and walks away.

We let him go. The place isn't that big. He can find his own way out. It's only an IRDHouse, for goodness sake.

We begin inspecting the little computer. It has a tiny little screen built into it, and a tiny little keyboard for us to enter our programs.

We turn it on.

Figure 9-1 The IRD Toy Object Builder screen

Figure 9-2 The IRD Toy Object Builder's second screen

There's a loud, deep hum. The walls shake a little bit. Then the noise dies out as the airplane flying overhead disappears.

The computer has its own tiny little hum. We tap on it lightly.

Still humming.

We pound on it violently.

The hum stops and the little screen lights up. There's some writing on it. It says, "Figure 9-1."

We can't find the enter key, but we find one with an arrow pointing left. Maybe that's it. We press it, and the screen changes. It now has the words "Figure 9-2" at the bottom.

Great! We can begin describing the classes. Um, what classes? What is it we're trying to do? Shouldn't we have some sort of goal in mind?

Of course! The racquetball court. This computer has to control the racquetball court. But how? Hmmm. Maybe we're not ready to write our program yet. Let's see, there must be the standard chalkboard around here somewhere. Maybe on the wall inside the racquetball court? No, that's a dumb place. How about out here in the hallway? Sure, there it is.

We approach it. Let's see . . . We need to build a program that controls the racquetball courts. So that should be our first class of objects: the Court class. And we need some methods, of course.

We stop a moment. This is pretty important. We'd better have a new section header.

Chapter 9

The User of the Class

We realize that this class has to be used by someone or something. More likely, something: the computer program. But does that make sense?

Sure. Some part of the computer program, probably the main, must use this class. Chances are, we'll write our main to make a new object of this class, do something with it, and then get rid of it, and finally finish. So there is indeed a user of this class: the main part of the program.

But since we're the ones writing the main, we need to know how to use the class. That's easy, because we'll be building the class ourselves.

Or will we? This time we will, but we recall how at work there are lots of people working on the IRD programs, and some people build classes that other people have to use in their programs. So maybe we should take the same approach to reusability here. After all, You never know who else may end up having to use your class descriptions—and any other part of your program, for that matter.

So let's be very, very careful. We'll try to make this class easy to use.

In the Public Eye

Maybe that's why we had all that public and private stuff earlier on. The other people who use our class can call the public methods. That's how they access the class.

We've written programs that have public attributes, too, but it seems like someone told us that we really shouldn't do that. So let's keep the

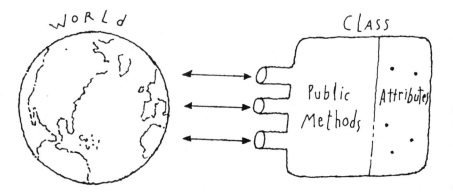

Figure 9-3 The beginnings of the Big Picture

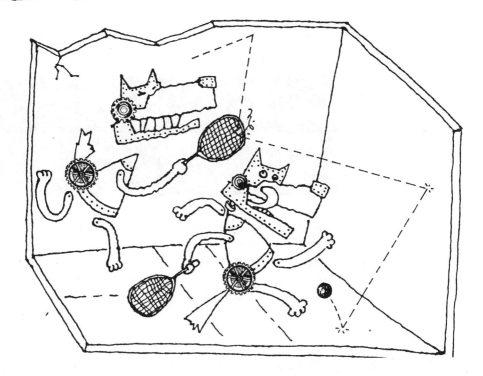

attributes private, and let the user access the class only through the public methods. We draw this idea on the chalkboard and call it Figure 9-3. The world can only access the class through its public functions.

But that's a bit abstract, so let's try and draw something a little closer to home. Then, in a little while, we'll redraw this figure with real-live names of the class and attributes. Then it'll make a little more sense.

Let's go directly to the first class in the problem at hand. What is it? The big class describing the entire racquetball court: the Court class.

What does this class do? First, we remind ourselves, it exists only inside the computer attached to the door. It simulates the real racquetball court, but it still exists only inside the computer.

And how does it simulate it? It keeps track of who's inside the court.

So what public methods do we have? Well, we can ask it who's in the court. We can tell it someone just left the room. We can tell it someone else just entered the room.

We could even get fancy: Since it keeps track of who's in the room, it could tell us if there are already two people in the room, and when a third person tries to enter, it could signal an alarm.

It could do all kinds of cool stuff. So let's list them on the chalkboard. We'll use computer-like names for all these methods:

```
Class: Court
public methods
    PersonEnters(name)
    PersonLeaves(name)
    CountPeople()
```

The word "person" can refer to humans and IRDs alike. After all, IRDs are people, too.

We look over our handiwork. Hey, it's pretty good! We've got a whole group of public methods for accessing this class.

But wait. Something's missing. Of course: the constructor and destructor. We'll add those shortly.

Behind the Scenes

These are just the public methods, of course. Really, that's all the user should have to worry about. The stuff going on inside the class is our problem, not the user's. All the user should have to care about is what the public methods are and how to use them.

We have to worry about the private stuff, the stuff inside, since we're developing the class. So let's work on that part.

First, the attributes. What things does this class have to remember and keep track of?

Well, the names of the people. And since there are two people, we can have two names listed.

Maybe we should keep a count, too. That way, when the user calls the CountPeople method, we can just look at the count attribute, rather than try and figure out how many of the two name slots have names in them. Of course, we could just count the names when that happens.

Hmm . . . Both approaches have their good and bad points. Let's go with the first. We'll maintain a Count attribute.

So we rewrite the class like this:

```
Class: Court
private attributes
    FirstName
    SecondName
    Count
public methods
    PersonEnters(name)
    PersonLeaves(name)
    CountPeople()
    Constructor
    Destructor
```

Is That All?

We look at the board for a moment and try and decide if that's everything. Hmm. What if we want to know the names of the people inside? Maybe we should add a couple more methods.

But first, let's divide up the public methods. Some are for changing information, like who's inside, and others are for getting information, like how many people are in the court.

So let's put the ones for changing information first, and the ones for getting information after that. We'll include some comments for our own purposes, just for keeping it straight. We rewrite it, including the new methods for finding out the names of the people:

```
class: Court
private attributes
    FirstName
    SecondName
    Count
```

continued on next page

continued from previous page

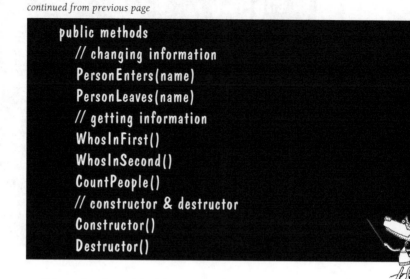

```
public methods
    // changing information
    PersonEnters(name)
    PersonLeaves(name)
    // getting information
    WhosInFirst()
    WhosInSecond()
    CountPeople()
    // constructor & destructor
    Constructor()
    Destructor()
```

We notice how big it's getting, but we're starting to feel pretty confident we can handle it.

The Secret Methods

Now let's think a little about some of this stuff. First, let's look at the PersonEnters method. The first time that function does its thing, it'll put the name in the FirstName slot. The second time, it'll put the name in the SecondName slot.

What if the first person leaves and someone else comes in to take his or her place? Then the PersonEnters will put the new name in the FirstName slot.

But what if it was the second person who left? Then there would be an empty space in the SecondName slot.

And what if they both left? Then it would be sort of arbitrary.

Hmm. It's almost as if we need another method to figure out which slot to put the next name in. But is that something the user needs? Not at all.

Hey! That's it! We'll have another method to do just that—figure out what the next available slot is, if there even is one. But it won't be a public method! Only the other methods can call this method. The users in the real world won't have access to this method. It's a private method. Cool!

We add this one private method, GetSlot, to the list, and we have our final class.

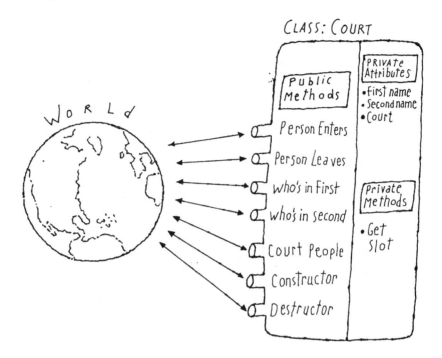

Figure 9-4 The Big Picture

```
class: Court
private attributes
    FirstName
    SecondName
    Count
private methods
    GetSlot()
```

It's now ready to be programmed. But first let's step back and look at the big picture.

The Big Picture

Next, we can draw a picture like the one in Figure 9-3, only we can have some actual names. So we redraw it and call it Figure 9-4.

We see in this picture that the users of the world who use our class are only allowed to access it through its public methods. The public methods are like little pipes through which information is exchanged. The users can either send information into the pipes, or get information out of the pipes. But they can only go through these pipes.

Why does it have to be that way? Why shouldn't they be allowed to directly access the private attributes? After all, we can write code that lets the users do that.

We think about it and think about it, and finally come up with an idea. At the office, we have lots of people working together, using each other's classes. But we remember hearing the story of how Bill built a really cool class describing the IRD's mouth. The class worked great, but occasionally it would screw up and incorrectly taste food. That was Bill's fault. He had an error in his code.

The problem was that it was storing the wrong foods in the wrong place. That is, he screwed up when he put together the attributes. But he was able to fix it without too much trouble.

Fortunately, though, he provided a pretty good public interface, and that didn't have to be changed. So when he made his changes of the attributes, the users didn't have to worry about changing their programs. The public interface didn't change, only some private stuff. So as far as the users knew, suddenly one day the thing started functioning correctly, and they didn't have to change their code. It was Bill who had to stay up all night.

And that's why we have public and private stuff. Interesting.

Program Section

Now let's try to actually design some C++ programs that do this Court class thing.

Before we do it, though, let's let the author step in for a quick note about reality. He says

A WORD FROM THE AUTHOR

Slipping back to reality, this program may not seem very realistic. However, it is. This program really could function on a small computer keeping track of who's inside a racquetball court. But there's one difference: The one here has a main()

in it that just creates the new court, calls some of the Court public methods, outputs some stuff, and deletes the object.

In real life, however, this program would probably create the object initially, and just sit there, waiting to be turned off. While it's sitting there, though, the public methods would get activated by real-world events. For instance, a person wishing to enter the court might insert a magnetic badge into a reader, which would detect his identity. This reader would then send an electronic message to the computer, signaling the PersonEnters() method. The PersonEnters() method would return to the user (that is, return to the reader) whether there is room in the court for another person.

There might also be an electronic display above the door listing the names of the people inside the court. Whenever a person enters or leaves, the class attributes Name1 and Name2 would get changed appropriately, and at the same time this electronic display would get activated.

This, in fact, demonstrates OOP under event-driven programming. Cool, huh?

Now back to our story . . .

Example 1: Strings

Before we can start writing the class, there's something we need to figure out how to do: store names of people, whether they're humans or IRDs.

We consult the *IRD Programmer's Manual* about strings, and for once it's actually readable. It says that in most programming languages, including C++, a sequence of letters and numbers stored as characters is known as a *string*. Any time we say "string," we're referring to a string of characters.

For instance, these are strings:

- ABC
- Hello
- My name is Mitch
- 123 456

Strings can have spaces, just like the third and fourth examples. So that's what those are. So let's try and do it in C++.

Before we can use all the capabilities of strings in C++, we need to include someone else's program. The program to include is called string, and it comes with every C and C++ compiler. We put this line at the beginning of our program:

```
include <string.h>
```

To save a string inside the computer memory requires a little bit of effort in C++. That's because the whole thing takes up several memory locations (one location per character). To access it, we need a pointer to the first.

First, here's a pointer to a string:

```
char *str;
```

We realize that this is a pointer to a character. But the *IRD Programmer's Manual* assures us that it's okay. The pointer points to the first character, which is also pointing to the start of the string. So that's fine.

Now, how do we make a new string? We say new, just like this:

```
str = new char[50];
```

That sets aside some computer memory big enough for a string of length 50. If we anticipate larger strings, we'll need to use a larger number. But for storing the names of the people in the racquetball court, that should be plenty. (Actually, because of the way computers store strings, there's only room for a string of length 49, not 50. For now, we won't worry about this; but if you're curious, you can glance ahead to Sample 3, under "New Stuff: NULL Terminators.")

But that only sets aside the computer memory. We still have to fill it with the appropriate letters. To do that, we use a stand-alone function provided for us when we included STRING.H. Suppose we want to copy the string "My Favorite IRD." into this computer memory. Here's how we do it:

```
strcpy (str, "My Favorite IRD.");
```

That means, "Copy into string the stuff inside 'My Favorite IRD.'" With strcpy, the first parameter is always the destination, and the second parameter is always the source. And both parameters are either pointers to strings, or an actual string enclosed in quotes.

And that should do it.

We can put all this together into a sample program. Here it is in Listing 9-1.

Listing 9-1 My Favorite IRD

```
#include <string.h>
#include <iostream.h>

void main()
{
    char *str;

    str = new char[50];
    strcpy (str, "My Favorite IRD.");

    cout << str << endl;
}
```

The output looks like this:

```
My Favorite IRD.
```

Example 2: Parameters and Returns

Before we build the court class, we decide to look at a couple more is-
sues dealing with the parameters getting passed, and what the methods
return.

Many of the methods take no parameters, so they get an empty set
of parentheses for the parameter list. Some return nothing, so they get
the word "void" before them.

The PersonEnters and PersonLeaves methods take strings as parameters.

But there's a problem. To pass strings, we really have to pass pointers to the strings, like so:

```
void PersonLeaves(char *name);
```

The PersonEnters method works almost the same, except we want it
to return something to us—whether or not the person is allowed to enter. If there is no room, the person can't enter. Often functions like this
that return a yes or no are programmed to return a number, 1 for yes,
and 0 for no, like so:

```
int PersonEnters(char *name);
```

Then how do we handle the WhosInFirst and WhosInSecond methods? We need them to give back to us the names. The way we could do
that is to return a pointer to the string called name. That would work,
but there's a better way: We'll have them fill in a string for us. We'll call

the string a *buffer*, and we'll tell the methods about this buffer, and they will fill in the buffer with the appropriate names. Then we can do what we want with the buffer. In fact, since it's ours, we can even change it without worrying about messing up the names inside the class.

We pass a buffer just like we pass a string, because the buffer really is a string. We just won't know what characters are in it until after the WhosInFirst or WhosInSecond methods fill it.

So here's how we specify that these two methods take a string:

```
void WhosInFirst(char *buffer)
void WhosInSecond(char *buffer);
```

And we still need to figure out what the GetSlot method returns. (It takes no parameters, though.)

How about this: If it decides FirstName is available, it will return a 1. If instead it decides SecondName is available, it will return a 2. But if neither is available, what should it return? How about 0.

Example 3: The Court Class

So now we're ready. But first a word of caution: This class is big. So you may want to take it slowly through the next several pages. Here's what the class looks like:

```
class Court
{
private:
    // Attributes
    char *FirstName;
    char *SecondName;
    int Count;

    // Private methods
    int GetSlot();
public:
    // Public methods

    // Constructor & Destructor

    Court();
    Court(char *First, char *Second);
    ~Court();

    // Changing information
    int PersonEnters(char *name);
    void PersonLeaves(char *name);
```

```
    // Getting information
    void WhosInFirst(char *buffer);
    void WhosInSecond(char *buffer);
    int CountPeople();
};
```

As we look over the code we just wrote, we realize we included two constructors. That's fine; we're doing that "overloading" thing. One constructor is for when we want to create a new Court object while nobody's in the court, and the other is for when we want to start out with some people in the court. When it comes time to build our main(), we'll look at both possibilities.

Example 4: Methods

Now we're ready to start writing the code for the methods. This is gonna get long.

First, we aren't going to put the code inside the class definition as we generally did before. The main reason is to keep things readable for us humans.

So let's go through the code, method by method.

First, the constructors. The first one takes no parameters, and needs to initialize the two name strings. (Remember, constructors do initialization stuff.) It also has to initialize the Count attribute, which keeps careful track of how many people are in the court. (We can't assume the Count attribute will start out at 0. Generally, it's best to initialize all variables, even if they start out at 0.)

So here's what it looks like:

```
Court::Court()
{
    FirstName = new char[50];
    SecondName = new char[50];
    strcpy (FirstName,"");
    strcpy (SecondName,"");
    Count = 0;
}
```

Notice the lines

```
strcpy (FirstName,"");
strcpy (SecondName,"");
```

We need to include these because when the computer sets aside the FirstName and SecondName space, it doesn't clear it out. That means there could be any strange set of characters inside it, perhaps something left over from when another program ran. But this tells us to make the two strings equal to zero-length strings (indicated by the pair of quote marks). The computer knows how to handle this strange concept, and will take care of things for us, making it essentially seem like there are no names in the strings.

The second constructor also has to initialize the two strings, since only one constructor will get called for each object. The difference is that this constructor fills in the strings with the supplied names.

So it looks like:

```
Court::Court(char *First, char *Second)
{
    FirstName = new char[50];
    SecondName = new char[50];
    strcpy (FirstName, First);
    strcpy (SecondName, Second);
    Count = 2;
}
```

Notice that this time we're initializing Count to 2, since we're starting out with two people in the court.

Next is the destructor. This code has to clean up the stuff that took place while the class was created. In this case, we have to delete the strings. (If we don't, it's possible they will stick around in computer memory and the memory will gradually get used up until the computer

can't work anymore.) Note that we *only* delete the things that we had a New statement for, and in this case, that's FirstName and SecondName. Here's how we do it:

```
Court::~Court()
{
    delete FirstName;
    delete SecondName;
}
```

The PersonLeaves routine is a tad more involved. It has to figure out which slot the person leaving is in—FirstName or SecondName. Then it has to delete the name. Finally, it subtracts one from Count, since Count is keeping track of how many people are in the court.

How does it delete the name? Simply by copying blanks into either FirstName or SecondName.

So here are the steps, in semi-English:

if name matches FirstName,
    remove FirstName
else if name matches SecondName,
    remove SecondName
end-if
subtract 1 from Count

Notice that if the name doesn't match the FirstName, we're not automatically assuming it matches the SecondName. We're still comparing it to the second name. This is in case someone passes to the PersonLeaves routine a name of somebody who is not inside the court.

But how does it know which string to use, FirstName or SecondName? By using a function called strcmp.

So here's what the code looks like. Notice the close similarity to the semi-English thing above.

```
void Court::PersonLeaves(char *name)
{
    if (strcmp(FirstName, name) == 0)
    {
        strcpy(FirstName,"");
        Count--;
    }
    else if (strcmp(SecondName, name) == 0)
    {
        strcpy(SecondName,"");
        Count--;
    }
}
```

Notice the lines with the strcmp function. They are comparing the results of the function call to 0. This is because if strcmp returns a 0, it means the strings match.

Before we can do the PersonEnters method, remember we need the GetSlot method to figure out which position to put the person in. The GetSlot method will first check if the FirstName slot is empty, and if so, return a 1. But if it's not empty, it will check the SecondName slot. If that one is open, it will return a 2. Otherwise, if will return a 0, meaning no slots are open.

Let's write that in semi-English:

```
if FirstName is available
    return 1
else if SecondName is available
    return 2
else
    return 0
end-if
```

We can pretty much do a direct translation to C++ from that. But how do we know if a slot is available? We strcmp ("string-compare") it to the empty string, "".

Here's what the routine looks like, then:

```
int Court::GetSlot()
{
    if (strcmp(FirstName,"") == 0
    {
        return 1;
    }
    else if (strcmp(SecondName,"") == 0)
    {
        return 2;
    }
    else
    {
        return 0;
    }
}
```

And now we're ready to add the PersonEnters method. All it has to do is call the GetSlot method, and if that method returns a 1, copy the name into slot 1 and add 1 to Count. If it returns a 2, copy the name into slot 2 and add 1 to Count. If it returns a 0, there's no room, so don't copy anything.

If the method manages to copy the name into either FirstName or SecondName, it should return a 1 for yes. If it can't copy the name into a slot, it should return a 0 for no.

In semi-English, that thought process looks like this:

```
if GetSlot returns 1
    copy into slot 1
    add 1 to Count
    return 1
else if GetSlot returns 2
    copy into slot 2
    add 1 to Count
    return 1
else
    return 0
end-if
```

But we should look at this to make sure there are no problems. Suppose we call GetSlot, and it gives us a 1. That means we copy the name into slot 1 and return. Putting the return here means we'll return from the method immediately. The same process then goes for slot 2, and finally, for slot 0.

But there's a catch. Do we really want to call GetSlot three times, just to find out there's no room? That's what would happen if GetSlot returns 0. It would call it the first time, see it's not 1, and bounce to the "else if GetSlot returns 2" part. That means it calls GetSlot a second time. Then it would bounce to the "else if GetSlot returns 0" part, calling GetSlot a third time.

Instead, let's make a local variable called Slot, and call GetSlot only once, storing the number it returns in this variable called Slot.

So it looks like this:

```
int Court::PersonEnters(char *name)
{
    int Slot;

    Slot = GetSlot();
    if (Slot == 1)
    {
        strcpy(FirstName, name);
        Count++;
        return 1;
    }
    else if (Slot == 2)
```

continued on next page

continued from previous page

```
    {
        strcpy(SecondName, name);
        Count++;
        return 1;
    }
    else
    {
        return 0;
    }
}
```

And that's all the methods that change information. Now let's do the methods that are for getting information. They're a bit less involved.

First are the WhosInFirst and WhosInSecond methods. They're very similar. Remember, we already decided we'll be passing a pointer to a buffer, so all we have to do is copy the appropriate string into a buffer. That's accomplished using the strcpy function, like so:

```
void Court::WhosInFirst(char *buffer)
{
    strcpy (buffer, FirstName);
}

void Court::WhosInSecond(char *buffer)
{
    strcpy (buffer, SecondName);
}
```

The CountPeople function isn't too bad...

```
int Court::CountPeople()
{
    return Count;
}
```

And that's the whole class! Let's build a main and put the whole thing together into one big program.

Here's the whole program, Listing 9-2, with a sample main.

Listing 9-2 The Whole Program

```
#include <string.h>
#include <iostream.h>

class Court
{
private:
    // Attributes
```

```
    char *FirstName;
    char *SecondName;
    int Count;

    // Private methods
    int GetSlot();
public:
    // Public methods

    // Constructor & Destructor

    Court();
    Court(char *First, char *Second);
    ~Court();

    // Changing information
    int PersonEnters(char *name);
    void PersonLeaves(char *name);

    // Getting information
    void WhosInFirst(char *buffer);
    void WhosInSecond(char *buffer);
    int CountPeople();
};

Court::Court()
{
    FirstName = new char[50];
    SecondName = new char[50];
    strcpy (FirstName,"");
    strcpy (SecondName,"");
    Count = 0;
}

Court::Court(char *First, char *Second)
{
    FirstName = new char[50];
    SecondName = new char[50];
    strcpy (FirstName, First);
    strcpy (SecondName, Second);
    Count = 2;
}

Court::~Court()
{
    delete FirstName;
    delete SecondName;
}
```

continued on next page

continued from previous page

```
void Court::PersonLeaves(char *name)
{
    if (strcmp(FirstName, name) == 0)
    {
        strcpy(FirstName,"");
        Countñ;
    }
    else if (strcmp(SecondName, name) == 0)
    {
        strcpy(SecondName,"");
        Count--;
    }
}

int Court::GetSlot()
{
    if (strcmp(FirstName,"") == 0)
    {
        return 1;
    }
    else if (strcmp(SecondName,"") == 0)
    {
        return 2;
    }
    else
    {
        return 0;
    }
}

int Court::PersonEnters(char *name)
{
    int Slot;

    Slot = GetSlot();
    if (Slot == 1)
    {
        strcpy(FirstName, name);
        Count++;
        return 1;
    }
    else if (Slot == 2)
    {
        strcpy(SecondName, name);
        Count++;
        return 1;
    }
    else
    {
        return 0;
    }
}
```

```
void Court::WhosInFirst(char *buffer)
{
    strcpy (buffer,FirstName);
}

void Court::WhosInSecond(char *buffer)
{
    strcpy (buffer,SecondName);
}

int Court::CountPeople()
{
    return Count;
}

void main()
{
    Court *Original;

    // We need a buffer for when we get the names, so here it is:
    char *buffer;
    buffer = new char[50];

    cout << "Initializing Original with parameters!" << endl;
    Original = new Court;          // Create a new Court object.

    // Put some names in the court, and check
    // how many people are there.

    cout << endl << "Adding some names!" << endl;
    Original->PersonEnters("Scott");
    cout << "Number of people in Original = ";
    cout << Original->CountPeople() << endl;
    Original->PersonEnters("IRD");
    cout << "Number of people in Original = ";
    cout << Original->CountPeople() << endl;

    // List the people

    cout << endl << "Listing People!" << endl;
    Original->WhosInFirst(buffer);
    cout << "First has " << buffer << endl;
    Original->WhosInSecond(buffer);
    cout << "Second has " << buffer << endl;

    // Remove one person, then remove
    // someone who's not there.

    cout << endl << "Removing some people!" << endl;
    Original->PersonLeaves("Scott");
    cout << "Number of people in Original = ";
    cout << Original->CountPeople() << endl;
```

continued on next page

continued from previous page

```
cout << endl << "Remove someone not there!" << endl;
Original->PersonLeaves("John");
cout << "Number of people in Original = ";
cout << Original->CountPeople() << endl;

// Clean up

cout << endl << "Cleaning up!" << endl;
delete Original;
}
```

Wow! That's a long program! But remember, we looked at each piece as we built it up; so we should be able to see the program in those separate pieces, rather than a million lines of code all jumbled together. (In fact, that's an insider's secret. Programmers won't always admit it, but they view programs in terms of pieces, in the same way that we built up this program in pieces. That keeps everyone from getting confused!)

Anyway, here's the output for that program:

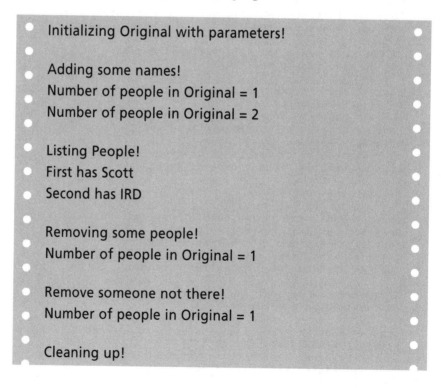

Initializing Original with parameters!

Adding some names!
Number of people in Original = 1
Number of people in Original = 2

Listing People!
First has Scott
Second has IRD

Removing some people!
Number of people in Original = 1

Remove someone not there!
Number of people in Original = 1

Cleaning up!

Remember that Original is a pointer, so we need to use the -> notation when we access the different methods. Remember too that since it's a pointer, we use the new and delete operators.

Notice we didn't use the second form of the constructor, the one that takes a parameter. You might try modifying the main so it instead uses the second constructor. (Here's a hint: Add some parameters to the statement where we create a new Court object.)

Don't Panic

Whew! This has been a rather long chapter, but we made it! Don't panic if you feel a tad overwhelmed. If you don't feel overwhelmed, great! Either way, congratulations on making it this far.

10
YOUR BOSS
WILL GIVE
YOU ARRAYS

It's Monday morning, and already we're ready to go home for the week-end. But, unfortunately, we can't. So we may as well make the best of it.

Our IRD barks and raises his paw. He's trying to deliver a message. We look him in the face and say, "Who is it?"

"It's B.B. Have a little respect."

"Hi, B.B. What's up?"

"I'm thinking about giving you the week off. You can leave at noon today. And I'm gonna give you something to think about: arrays."

"A raise!"

"No, I didn't say a raise. I said arrays."

"Oh. What are arrays?"

"A raise is a thing you get when you work hard."

"No, no. What are arrays?"

"Oh, I thought you said a raise. I honestly don't know. I'm not a com-puter programmer. I think it might have something to do with a whole group of variables, though. Better check with Linda. She's been pro-moted, you know. She now puts R.G. after her name. She's an official Resident Genius. She even carries the card." The IRD clicks. I guess B.B. hung up.

Wow! We can go home if we figure out what arrays are. At least we now know how to spell them. We grab our handy-dandy dictionary and begin looking up the word, when it dawns on us that even if we remember what the real word means, it's probably totally different from the computerese word. We put the dictionary back down and try to keep from remembering what it means in real life. But it's hopeless. The definition slips into our mind. We try to ignore it, but we can't. An array is like a grid. Hmmm . . . Better go visit Linda.

Monday = An Array of Blahs

We head to Linda's office, and she's already hard at work at her computer. We ask her what she's working on.

"I'm working on the budget class to handle how much money the IRD has each month to spend on IRDFood. I'm giving the IRD the ability to budget for 24 months. That means I need 24 attributes for this class, each one holding a dollar amount."

"That sounds fine and all, but I have some questions. Could you hold your thoughts for a moment?" we ask.

"Sure! What's the question?"

"What's an array?"

"Well, it's a whole group of variables of the same type. For instance, I need a whole group of dollar-amounts—24 of them, to be exact. I could define the class to have 24 separate attributes, each for a single month. But I can actually combine all 24 into one attribute. I can call it an array of 24 dollar-amounts."

She hops up and approaches the chalkboard, and writes something like this:

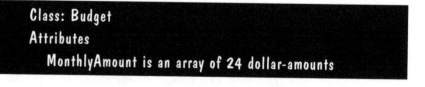

```
Class: Budget
Attributes
    MonthlyAmount is an array of 24 dollar-amounts
```

"There!" she says. "We have a class with 24 attributes, each representing a separate month. When we need to access a single one of those, we just say the name of the array, MonthlyAmount, and follow it with what we call an index—that is, a number from 0 to 23, which specifies which item in the array we want to use. Like this." She writes this on the board:

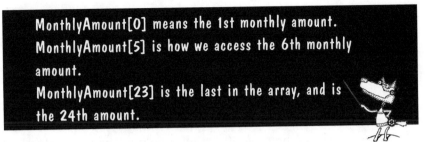

> MonthlyAmount[0] means the 1st monthly amount.
> MonthlyAmount[5] is how we access the 6th monthly
> amount.
> MonthlyAmount[23] is the last in the array, and is
> the 24th amount.

"Notice," she says, "that the first index is 0. And since there are 24 total, the last index is 23."

We ask if there is any other reason to do this than to save typing when we enter the class name.

"Oh, there's one big reason. When we specify the index, we can actually use a variable to specify it. We can even put it in a loop." She writes the following on the chalkboard:

> For an index starting at 0 and ending at 23,
>   Get the MonthlyAmount[index]
> end-for

She says, "This means we'll go through a loop from 0 to 23, and set the initial values, one by one. Sure, we could have typed in a whole series of 24 statements, one after the other, to read each thing in one by one. But this is a lot easier. And imagine how much you'd need to type if you had 5,000 of something to keep track of, instead of just two dozen!"

Thinking about leaving at noon, we tell her that's pretty cool. We stand up and say thanks.

"Wait, there's more!" she says.

We politely sit back down and glance at our watch. It's 11:45.

Plethora the Pointer

Linda resumes talking. "Remember when you learned about pointers this weekend?"

We consider asking how she knew that, but decide not to. We're not sure we want to know the answer. She might prove that we really *are* living in a textbook, and that would be pretty traumatic.

"Well? Do you remember learning about pointers?"

We think back to our walk down the strangely appropriate street and our thoughts about addresses. We nod.

"And remember how you can specify that one variable points to another?" Again, we nod.

"Well, arrays have a built-in pointer. We saw earlier that we can access each member by specifying the name followed by an index in brackets. If we refer only to the name, that's actually a pointer to the first element in the array. For instance, we saw how to access the elements 0, 5, and 23 of our MonthlyAmount array." She approaches the chalkboard and writes this:

> This is a pointer to the first element:
> MonthlyAmount

She then says, "But this example shows how we represent a pointer to the first element in the array. And do you know how we can specify a pointer to the second element?"

Before we have time to fudge an answer, she says, "We just add 1 to the pointer." She writes the following:

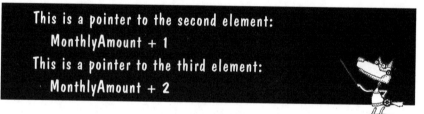

> This is a pointer to the second element:
> MonthlyAmount + 1
> This is a pointer to the third element:
> MonthlyAmount + 2

"The second example in this figure points to the third element," she says. "Pretty cool, huh?"

We glance at our watch. 11:55. "Cool."

We stand up.

"Sit down," she snaps. Then she grins.

Size

A thought suddenly occurs to us. What if the array contains objects that take up several memory addresses? Wouldn't that screw up adding 1 to the pointer? Linda reads our mind. "No, that won't be a problem at all. The C++ language knows how to adjust when we add 1 to pointer: It

will automatically add 'one' of the right-sized things. So, let's move on to the Program Section for some real-live examples!"

Program Section

Linda stays with us for the Program Section, for once. We ignore our hunger pangs, and continue.

Example 1: Array of Integers

She says, "Let's look at an example of an array of integers. Here it is!" She writes the following program (Listing 10-1).

Listing 10-1 Arrays Example 1

```
#include <iostream.h>

void main()
{
    int a[10];          // a is an array of size 10.
                        // That means its elements have
                        // indexes 0 thru 9.
    int i;
```

continued on next page

continued from previous page

```
cout << "Please enter ten numbers,";
cout << " pressing return after each." << endl;

for (i=0; i<10; i++)     // Notice its < size.
{
    cin >> a[i];
}

cout << endl << "Here's what you entered:" << endl;
for (i=0; i<10; i++)
{
    cout << a[i] << endl;
}
}
```

We type in the above program and run it. (For this sample output we entered the numbers 10, 15, 23, 65, 21, 65, 76, 27, 43, and 20.) Here's what we see:

```
Please enter ten numbers, pressing return after each.
10
15
23
65
21
65
76
27
43
20

Here's what you entered:
10
15
23
65
```

```
21
65
76
27
43
20
```

Example 2: Arrays of Objects

Linda erases the board. "Now," she says, "let's look at an example that uses arrays of objects. In this example we make a tiny little class and build an array of it. We then step through the elements of the array, the first time calling SetLevel to set the value for each object in the array, and the second time calling GetLevel for each object in the array. Since we need to call a method to store the level (the SetLevel method) we need a temporary storage variable to read in the level. Take a look at the program (Listing 10-2)."

Listing 10-2

```cpp
#include <iostream.h>

class Bark
{
private:
    int Level;
public:
    int GetLevel()
    { return Level; }
    void SetLevel(int Set)
    { Level = Set; }
};

void main()
{
    Bark AllMyDogs[5];
    int storage;
    int i;

    cout << "Please enter 5 barklevels,";
    cout << " pressing return after each." << endl;
```

continued on next page

continued from previous page

```
for (i=0; i<5; i++)      // Notice its < size.
{
    cin >> storage;
    AllMyDogs[i].SetLevel(storage);
}

cout << endl << "Here's what you entered:" << endl;
for (i=0; i<5; i++)
{
    cout << AllMyDogs[i].GetLevel() << endl;
}
}
```

Here's the output:

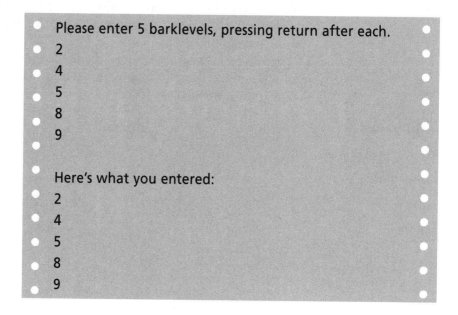

```
Please enter 5 barklevels, pressing return after each.
2
4
5
8
9

Here's what you entered:
2
4
5
8
9
```

Example 3: Pointers in Arrays

"This next example, Listing 10-3," says Linda, "demonstrates the concept of pointers in arrays. We'll first see an example of an array of integers; then, in Example 4, we'll see an example of an array of Bark class objects."

Listing 10-3

```
#include <iostream.h>

void main()
{
    int a[5], i;

    for (i=0; i<5; i++)
    {
        a[i] = i*2;      // Fill the array with 0,2,4,6,8
    }

    for (i=0; i<5; i++)
    {
        cout << "a+" << i << " points to ";
        cout << "element # " << i << endl;
        cout << "and contains ";
        cout << *(a+i) << endl << endl;
    }
}
```

And here's the output:

```
a+0 points to element # 0
and contains 0

a+1 points to element # 1
and contains 2

a+2 points to element # 2
and contains 4

a+3 points to element # 3
and contains 6

a+4 points to element # 4
and contains 8
```

Example 4: AllMyDogs

"Notice that this example," says Linda, "is really the same as Example 2, except we're pointing out the fact that AllMyDogs is a pointer—bad grammar and all. We'll call it Listing 10-4."

Listing 10-4

```
#include <iostream.h>

class Bark
{
private:
    int Level;
public:
    int GetLevel()
    { return Level; }
    void SetLevel(int Set)
    { Level = Set; }
};

void main()
{
    Bark AllMyDogs[5];
    int storage;
    int i;

    cout << "Please enter 5 barklevels,";
    cout << " pressing return after each." << endl;

    for (i=0; i<5; i++)     // Notice its < size.
    {
        cin >> storage;
        (*(AllMyDogs+i)).SetLevel(storage);
    }

    cout << endl << "Here's what you entered:" << endl;
    for (i=0; i<5; i++)
    {
        cout << (*(AllMyDogs+i)).GetLevel() << endl;
    }
}
```

Here's the output:

```
Please enter 5 barklevels, pressing return after each.
2
4
```

```
5
8
9

Here's what you entered:
2
4
5
8
9
```

"Notice the awkward notation," she continues, "used here to access the elements in the array. But it works. Probably the form in Example 2 is better, but you can do it this way, too. Also notice we needed another set of parentheses. How did I know to do that? Because the first time I wrote this program, which was before you came here, I left out the inner parentheses, and the compiler gave me an error. So I added them, and it worked just fine. I think the author had the exact same thing happen to him, too."

"The author?" we ask. "The author of what?"

"This book we're in."

"Goodness," we mumble under our breath. "We're starting to believe her. It's time to get out of this place!"

We go home and forget about work for a while.

Part 3
The Dog's
Favorite Entrees—
A Sampling

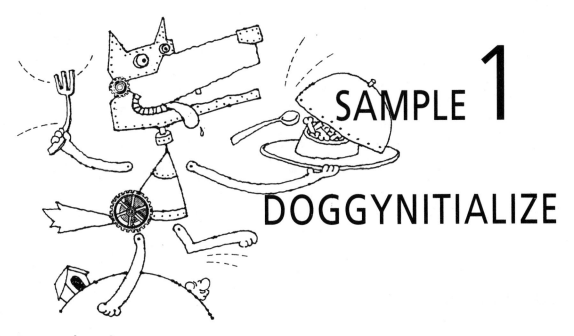

SAMPLE 1

DOGGYNITIALIZE

Introduction

C++ is big. The idea behind Part 3, is for us to look at some different aspects of C++ and build on what we've seen so far. What better way than to dive in and start writing programs for our IRD?

But first, a few remarks.

This section is a little different than the others. The emphasis here is on actual program examples rather than on the ideas behind the programs. So we'll keep the text to a minimum, and mainly talk about things such as what the program does, how we're going to build it, and if there's anything in the program that we haven't seen in a previous chapter.

That means Part 3 is more of a hands-on approach to programming, since that's just as important as the background in Part 2.

But there's one more thing. Most people, when they learn a new language—whether it's a spoken language, a written language, or even a computer language—don't try to learn absolutely every aspect of the language, every word, every little nuance. If they did, they'd have to make an entire career out of learning the language.

And C++ is no exception. It's not nearly as big as a spoken language, and indeed it is possible to learn everything about it. But since we're just getting started, we'll try to look at as many parts of C++ as we can. Then, when we need them in our future work, we can look them up and review them. After all, most programmers keep their books handy, and don't try to memorize everything about the language or the computer. Rather, they remember and know the important stuff that they use on a daily basis, and when they need something more obscure, they look it up.

So that's the way we'll do it in Part 3. We've got the foundation, and we'll look at some new stuff, and that way we know that it's there. In the future, when we need it again, we can say, "Oh yeah, I remember doing that. I'll just look it up and refresh my memory."

Also, to make things a little easier to follow, we'll put new stuff in boxes.

So back to our story . . .

Building a Better Doggy

We're at home, looking at our IRD, thinking about what we might do to make him better. How might we improve him?

Well, there are all sorts of things we could do.

As we stare at our IRD, we realize we're gonna need a class that models the IRD in general.

We won't bother making some gigantic hierarchy of classes; for now, we'll keep it simple and have just one class. We know we can make a hierarchy; let's just make one basic class. That way, we can spend time concentrating on our other explorations. We can improve on it later, too, and even build a hierarchy then.

Since we only have one class for dogs, we'll just call it the Dog class.

Now we need some attributes and methods.

Let's list some ideas on our chalkboard. These can come off the top of our head, and we'll add more later if we need them:

> **First Ideas on Attributes for Dog Class**
> **Owner's Name:** A string of characters of, say, size 20.
> **Color:** An enum consisting of red, green, blue, yellow, pink, silver.
> **Size:** A number from 1 to 100.
> **Favorite food:** A string of characters of, say, size 20.
> Could be an enum, but a string provides more flexibility.

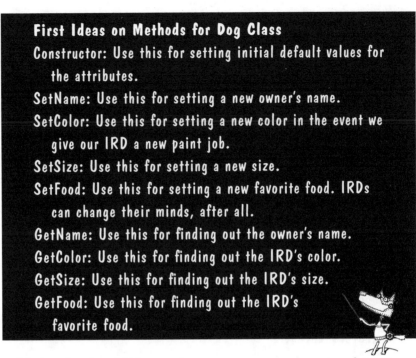

First Ideas on Methods for Dog Class

Constructor: Use this for setting initial default values for the attributes.

SetName: Use this for setting a new owner's name.

SetColor: Use this for setting a new color in the event we give our IRD a new paint job.

SetSize: Use this for setting a new size.

SetFood: Use this for setting a new favorite food. IRDs can change their minds, after all.

GetName: Use this for finding out the owner's name.

GetColor: Use this for finding out the IRD's color.

GetSize: Use this for finding out the IRD's size.

GetFood: Use this for finding out the IRD's favorite food.

Notice that in addition to the constructor, we have two basic types of methods: Those for setting attributes, and those for getting attributes. Often, we will have other methods, too, but generally we'll include these two basic types of methods for each attribute, if it's an attribute we want to give other classes access to. (Sometimes we don't want to, in which case we won't have these types of methods.)

SOMETHING NEW: DEFAULTS

We can provide what are called *defaults* in a parameter list for a method. Take a peek at the constructor in the code below, and you'll see that there are = signs in it. That means if we don't include that parameter, it defaults to the value provided. The main() demonstrates this. Note that if we provide a default for one parameter, the parameters that follow must also have defaults, and if we use one of the defaults; we must use the defaults for the rest of the parameters that follow. For instance, if we're using a method that has four parameters, all with defaults, and we only give two explicit parameters, those two go with the first two parameters in the method, and the remaining two get the defaults.

continued on next page

continued from previous page

SOMETHING NEW: OUR OWN HEADER FILE

We'll put the class definition in a file called DOG.H, and then when we write a program that needs that class, all it has to do is include the line

    #include 'dog.h'

at the beginning of the program. That'll make life a whole lot easier.

So here's the class, in Listing S1-1. Save it as DOG.H.

Listing S1-1 DOG.H

```
#include <string.h>

enum dogcolors {red, green, blue, yellow, pink, silver};

class Dog
{
    char name[20];
    dogcolors color;
    int size;
    char food[20];
public:
    Dog(char *theName = "NoName",
        dogcolors theColor = silver,
        int theSize = 10,
        char *theFood = "Pizza")
    {
        strncpy(name, theName, 20);
        color = theColor;
        size = theSize;
        strncpy (food, theFood, 20);
    }

    // functions for setting
    void SetName(char *theName)
    { strncpy(name, theName, 20); }

    void SetColor(dogcolors theColor)
    { color = theColor; }

    void SetSize(int theSize)
    { size = theSize; }

    void SetFood(char *theFood)
    { strncpy (food, theFood, 20); }
```

```
// functions for getting
void GetName(char *buffer)
{ strncpy (buffer, name, 20); }

dogcolors GetColor()
{ return color; }

int GetSize()
{ return size; }

void GetFood(char *buffer)
{ strncpy (buffer, food, 20); }
};
```

Take a close look at the constructor. The rest is really nothing new. Also, remember how we made this class. We thought about the attributes that were needed, and we listed them, and then we thought about what methods were needed for accessing and manipulating these attributes. We also included a constructor. We could also have included a destructor if necessary, and any other methods needed for this class.

Listing S1-2 is a sample program using this class. Notice we're including DOG.H at the beginning. Call this program SAMP1.CPP and go ahead and compile and run it.

Listing S1-2 SAMP1.CPP

```
#include "dog.h"

void main()
{
    Dog Scott;
    Dog Mitch("Mitch",green,10,"milkshake");
    char buffer[20];

    cout << "Scott:" << endl;
    Scott.GetName(buffer);
    cout << buffer << endl;
    cout << Scott.GetColor() << endl;
    cout << Scott.GetSize() << endl;
    Scott.GetFood(buffer);
    cout << buffer << endl << endl;

    cout << "Mitch:" << endl;
    Mitch.GetName(buffer);
    cout << buffer << endl;
```

continued on next page

continued from previous page

```
    cout << Mitch.GetColor() << endl;
    cout << Mitch.GetSize() << endl;
    Mitch.GetFood(buffer);
    cout << buffer << endl << endl;
}
```

The output of the program looks like this:

```
Scott:
NoName
5
10
Pizza

Mitch:
Mitch
1
10
milkshake
```

Notice that in the code we didn't provide any initial data for the object Scott, so all the parameters in the constructor took on their defaults: NoName, 5, 10, Pizza. However, with the object Mitch, we did include parameters: Mitch, green, 10, milkshake.

The Real World

Since your own programming needs probably don't involve robot dogs, each sample will have a section called The Real World. In each of these sections, we'll briefly look at other applications where the concepts in the sample can be used.

Often when you are modeling objects, you will want to provide default values in the methods. For instance, if you are writing a program that tracks customers' phone numbers and addresses, you may have a method called Save. Save may provide a default file name, such as PHONES.TXT.

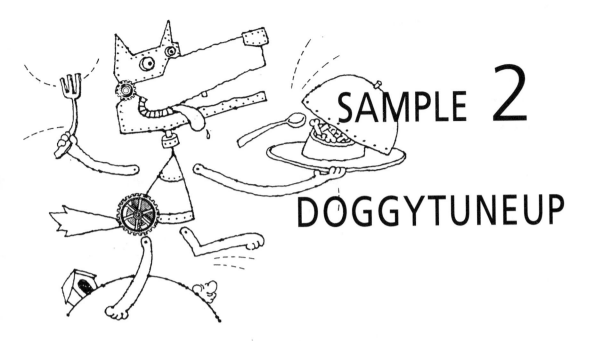

In this example we'll look at the process of passing to a function a pointer to a class.

NEW STUFF: MULTIPLE MODULES

As programs get bigger, it's generally a good idea to separate the different pieces into a different file, compile each separately, and finally link the different pieces together into one program. The specifics on how to do this depend on your compiler. (See the Introduction for more information on this.)

In this sample we'll be using multiple modules. We have two program modules, TUNEUP.CPP and SAMP2.CPP, along with two header files, DOG.H and TUNEUP.H.

Here's the tuneup function, in Listing S2-1. Save it in a file called TUNEUP.CPP.

Listing S2-1 TUNEUP.CPP

```
#include "dog.h"
#include "tuneup.h"

void tuneup (Dog *which)
{
```

continued on next page

continued from previous page

```
    int size;

    size = which->GetSize();
    which->SetSize(size+1);
}
```

This function takes a pointer to a Dog, and adds one to the dog's size. That's how a dog gets tuned up.

For our other module to access this function, it has to somehow know about it. So we make a new header file listing just enough information about it. Here it is, all "one lines" of it, in Listing S2-2; call it TUNEUP.H:

Listing S2-2 TUNEUP.H

```
void tuneup (Dog *which);
```

The purpose of this file is so other modules (such as the one below) can include it to find out about the tuneup function: that it exists, what its parameters are, and if it returns anything. It's sort of like "publishing" the function for others to use. This header makes the function official for all other modules to access.

This next code, Listing S2-3, demonstrates the tuneup function. You can call it SAMP2.CPP.

Listing S2-3 SAMP2.CPP

```
#include "dog.h"
#include "tuneup.h"
#include <iostream.h>

void main()
{
    Dog John("John",blue,20,"Icecream");

    cout << "Before tuneup..." << endl;
    cout << John.GetSize() << endl << endl;

    tuneup(&John);
    cout << "After tuneup..." << endl;
    cout << John.GetSize() << endl;
}
```

You can now compile the two modules, TUNEUP.CPP and SAMP2.CPP, and run the program. The output looks like this:

```
Before tuneup...
20

After tuneup...
21
```

Notice the tuneup function increased the size by 1, as expected.

The Real World

In the real world, there might be a computer at a tune-up center for cars. The program running inside this computer might have a class called Car, which contains basic information on the car being worked on. The mechanics using the program would enter this information in, and the information would go into attributes of an object of this class. A pointer to this Car object might then be passed on to a Tuneup object, which reads the attributes of the Car object, and figures out the optimum levels and settings for the car being worked on.

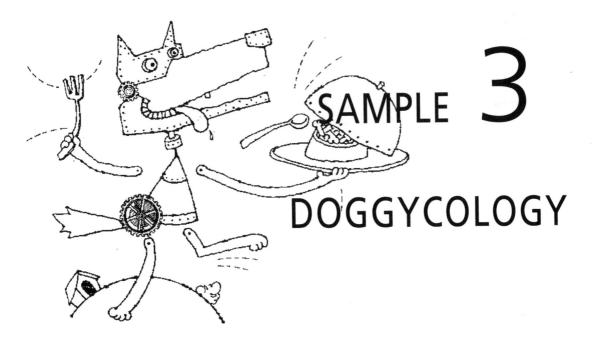

SAMPLE **3**

DOGGYCOLOGY

IRDs, like people, process food, so let's write a program that keeps track of how much food our IRD consumes.

NEW STUFF: FILE I/O

Often a program needs to save information so it can be used later. Variables work great for this, but not if we turn the computer off (or even rerun the program, for that matter). Fortunately, computers let us save information to a file, in much the same way that we save our program code to files. We (or some people, anyway) call this process *file I/O* (pronounced "file eye oh"), which stands for file input and output. (Those two rather annoying words have become a part of the wonderful world of computerese. The world may be better off without them, but such is life.)

The sample program here demonstrates file I/O. The process is almost exactly the same as using cin and cout. In fact, it *is* the same, except we tell the computer we're using a file instead and give it a name. Notice that we include FSTREAM.H instead of IOSTREAM.H, and have to create new objects of class ifstream and ofstream.

🦴 ifstream is for reading stuff *in* from a file.

🦴 ofstream is for writing stuff *out* to a file.

continued on next page

continued from previous page

We then read and write using << and >> (sometimes called the "insertion" and "extraction" operators, respectively; often called by less computerese people "less-less" and "greater-greater"). They work just like cout and cin, except the stuff gets written to or read from a file.

Here's the program . . . Take a special look at the ifstream and ofstream stuff. Notice the << and >> things behave much like the cin and cout equivalents.

First, the class; save it in a file called ACTIVITY.H (in Listing S3-1).

Listing S3-1 ACTIVITY.H

```
#include "dog.h"
class Activity
{
public:

    // To make life easier, we'll make it all public.  Some
    // would say it's okay, anyway.

    Dog *ourDog;     // Which dog we're working on
    int Running;     // How much running it did today
    int Eating;      // How much eating it did today
    int Pottying;    // How much pottying it did today

    Activity (Dog *which);
    void SetStuff(int Running = 10,
        int Eating = 10,
        int Pottying = 10);
    void ReadStuff();
    void WriteStuff();
};
```

We'll put the actual code separately, and here it is, in Listing S3-2. Type it in and save it as ACTIVITY.CPP.

Listing S3-2 ACTIVITY.CPP

```
// Here we use the alternate method of showing the code
// for the methods.

#include "activity.h"
#include <fstream.h>
```

```
Activity :: Activity (Dog *which)
{
    ourDog = which;
}

// We don't list the defaults for the parameters here;
// they only belong in the class definition.
void Activity :: SetStuff(int theRunning,
        int theEating,
        int thePottying)
{
    Running = theRunning;
    Eating = theEating;
    Pottying = thePottying;
}

void Activity :: WriteStuff()
{
    // often, we just use 'f' for the file variable.

    char name[20];
    ourDog->GetName(name);
    name[5] = '\0';         // just use the first four characters
                            // in the name. Gotta have a buffer of
                            // size 20, though, since the GetName
                            // function will write 20 no matter
                            // what.

    ofstream f(name);       // ofstream creates a file to write to
    f << Running << endl;
    f << Eating << endl;
    f << Pottying << endl;
}

void Activity :: ReadStuff()
{
    // often, we just use 'f' for the file variable.

    char name[20];
    ourDog->GetName(name);
    name[5] = '\0';         // just use the first four characters
                            // in the name. Gotta have a buffer of
                            // size 20, though, since the GetName
                            // function will write 20 no matter
                            // what.

    ifstream f(name);       // ifstream creates a file to read from
    f >> Running;
    f >> Eating;
    f >> Pottying;
}
```

Now a main, Listing S3-3. Save it as SAMP3.CPP.

Listing S3-3 SAMP3.CPP

```cpp
#include <iostream.h>
#include "activity.h"

void main()
{
    Dog Harry("Harry");        // The remaining parameters
                               // get the defaults
    Activity HarryAct(&Harry);

    HarryAct.SetStuff(5,4,3);
    cout << "Initially:" << endl;
    cout << HarryAct.Running << endl;
    cout << HarryAct.Eating << endl;
    cout << HarryAct.Pottying << endl;
    HarryAct.WriteStuff();
    cout << "Saved these values!" << endl << endl;

    HarryAct.SetStuff(1,2,1);
    cout << "New Values:" << endl;
    cout << HarryAct.Running << endl;
    cout << HarryAct.Eating << endl;
    cout << HarryAct.Pottying << endl << endl;

    HarryAct.ReadStuff();
    cout << "Read in previously saved values:" << endl;
    cout << HarryAct.Running << endl;
    cout << HarryAct.Eating << endl;
    cout << HarryAct.Pottying << endl << endl;
}
```

There are a couple of things to notice about this program. One thing is new, so we'll put it in a box.

NEW STUFF: NULL-TERMINATORS

When the computer stores a string of characters, it needs to keep track of how long the string is. The way it does it, then, is by storing the letters in sequence, and ending it with a number 0, called a *null-terminator*. That way, when we do a string function, or when we cout a string, the computer knows when to stop: It keeps printing characters until it comes to the null-terminator.

There's a difference, though, between the *character* 0 and the *number* 0. Every character actually is stored inside the computer's memory as a number, and there's a different number for each character. Although we generally don't need to know what these numbers specifically are, it won't hurt to see a couple: The character 0 is stored as 48, and the character 1 is stored as 49, and the character 2 is stored as 50.

The character A is stored as 65, and the character B is stored as 66. (Don't worry if you don't see much of a pattern, because there isn't much of one.)

Now we can look at the code, briefly. Notice the statements that look like

```
name[5] = '\0';
```

The \0 represents the null-terminator. So this statement means "Make the 5th entry in the string a null-terminator." That means we're forcing the string to end there, even though there may be stuff after the 5th position, if the name is long enough. The computer, then, will ignore anything after the 5th position, even if there's stuff there. And if the name was shorter than 4 characters, then there's a null-terminator before the 5th position, and that's the one the computer will see first. So, in that case, the computer will ignore anything after the first null-terminator, including the one we added in the fifth position.

So in a nutshell, we're chopping off the string after four characters by placing a null-terminator in the 5th position.

Later, we create the actual file. This is done by the line

```
ofstream f(name);
```

Since ofstream is a class, this means we're creating an object called F of class ofstream. The name of the file is passed as a parameter to ofstream's constructor. (Note that we don't actually see the class definition here; we can look at it, though, if we want; it's in the file called FSTREAM.H.)

Objects of class ofstream are files that we can save data into; objects of class ifstream are files we can read data from. (The o is for "output" and the i is for "input.")

Now you can compile the program. Just as in Sample 2, you have more than one program module, so you need to include both ACTIVITY.CPP and SAMP2.CPP in your project.

The output looks like this.

```
Initially:
5
4
3
Saved these values!

New Values:
1
2
1


Read in previously saved values:
5
4
3
```

Notice that we're saving the values to the text file, then changing the values. The only reason we're changing the values is so we can see that when we read the values back in, they really did return to their original values, rather than just stay that way.

The Real World

Almost every computer program requires file I/O. If you're writing an accounting package, you need to save all the general ledger account balances to a file. If you're developing a scientific application, you probably need to save lots of number and data to a file.

File I/O is one of the most common things in computer programs. Even IRDs need to save their data so they don't forget their names!

SAMPLE 4
DOGGYNETICS AND DOGMUTATIONS

We may get tired of making all the IRDs turn out the same, so let's bring some new classes of dogs into the picture. To do that, we'll derive some new classes from the dog class.

Notice that this is slightly different from the way we did it back in Chapter 5. Back then, we were modeling the pieces inside the IRD, and we made a hierarchy of classes based on those pieces. But here, we're starting with a single class representing an entire IRD, and from there making a hierarchy of classes, each representing a new kind of IRD. In both cases we have a hierarchy of classes, but each case models different things: pieces of the dog, or actual dogs.

We'll derive from the Dog class three new classes: FlyingDog, MegaDog, and CovertDog. The FlyingDog class adds flying capabilities to the IRD. The MegaDog is an IRD that can grow to enormous sizes. We'll derive even more from the general class CovertDog.

Figure S4-1 shows the hierarchy we'll create. From FlyingDog we derive one more class, WarpingDog, which has the ability to time-warp though the universe. From CovertDog class we'll derive two new classes, CIADog and WitnessDog.

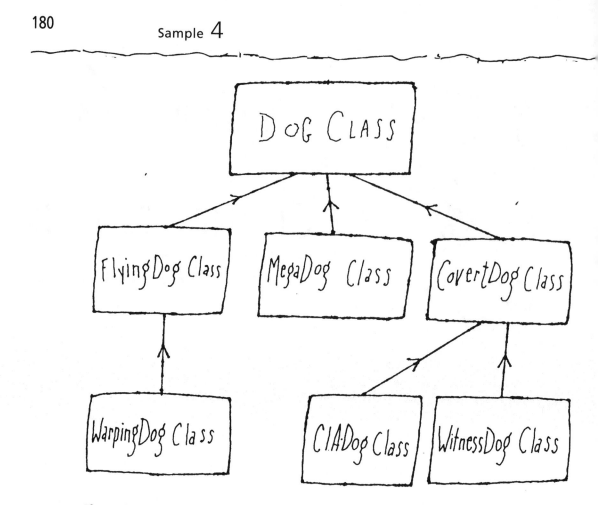

Figure S4-1 Genetic mutation hierarchy

THE ONE AND ONLY DEFINITION BOX

We've tried to avoid definition boxes like the plague, but this is one case where we can stand for one, because it's just another word for things we already know about.

The attributes and methods in a class are all members of the class.

So that's the word: member. Any attribute is a member. Any method is a member. It's just a convenient way of referring to all the attributes and methods: the members of the class.

NEW STUFF: PRIVATE AND PROTECTED METHODS AND ATTRIBUTES

We've already seen how methods and attributes can be public and private. Public means other classes can use them; private means other classes can't use them. But there's a problem with private: When we derive a new class from a base class, this new class can't manipulate or call the private attributes and methods in the base class. They're there; but they're not accessible. So the C++ designers have given us a third keyword for member privacy: protected.

If a member is protected, it is private to the outside world, but its derived classes can also see it. So it's sort of like private but accessible by the derived classes.

NEW STUFF: PRIVATE DERIVED CLASSES

In previous chapters we've seen how we can derive a class and have all the public members of the base class remain public. As mentioned above, the private members of the base class aren't accessible by the derived classes, whereas protected members are. The way we make a derived class behave this way is by attaching the word private before the base class name:

```
class derived : public base
{
}
```

We can, however, use the private in place of the word public, like so:

```
class derived : private base
{
}
```

If we do so, the public and protected members of the base class become private members of the derived class. As before, the public members of the base class aren't accessible by the derived class.

NEW STUFF: PARAMETERS, CONSTRUCTORS, AND BASE CLASSES

When we derive a new class, we can specify a new constructor. But we also get the constructor from the base class. However, only our derived class's constructor can access the base class' constructor. The code below demonstrates this and

continued on next page

continued from previous page

how it works. Note that only the constructor of the derived class can access the constructor of the base class. Notice also the strange way it's written out (that is, notice the strange *syntax*).

Listing S4-1 shows the rather long code for the sample classes mentioned above. They demonstrate these ideas. Type in the following and save it as XDOGS.H.

Listing S4-1 XDOGS.H

```
#include "dog.h"

// This IRD is a mutant that can fly
class FlyingDog : public Dog
{
    int HowHigh;
    int CruiseSpeed;
public:

    // Notice the parameters in the constructor.  The :
    // followed by the base class name is for specifying what
    // parameters to pass on to the constructor of the base
    // class.  We can send the same parameters we just received
    // (as we do with FlyingOwner and FlyingSize, or we can
    // send actual values, as we do with silver and "Steak."
    // This is because all FlyingDogs are silver and prefer
    // steak. (Seriously, that's the idea behind it... All the
    // objects of the derived class may have something in common,
    // and these common things can be explictly spelled out, as
    // they are here.)

    FlyingDog(char *FlyingOwner, int FlyingSize,
        int InitHeight, int InitSpeed ) : Dog(FlyingOwner,
        silver, FlyingSize, "Steak")
    {
        HowHigh = InitHeight;
        CruiseSpeed = InitSpeed;
    }
    GetHeight()
    { return HowHigh; }
    GetSpeed()
    { return CruiseSpeed; }
};
```

```
// This IRD is a mutant that can time-warp through the
// universe
class WarpingDog : public FlyingDog
{
private:
    int Parsecs;      // How far he's traveled
    int Time;         // How long he's traveled
public:
    // This constructor takes only the owner's name; all
    // warping dogs are size 5.  Even though we don't want
    // to do anything inside the constructor, we need to
    // include an empty set of curly braces.
    WarpingDog (char *WarpOwner) : FlyingDog(WarpOwner, 5, 0, 0)
    {
    }

    void Start()
    {
        Parsecs = 0;
        Time = 0;
    }
    void DoWarp()
    {
        Parsecs += 100;
        Time += 1000;
    }
    int GetParsecs()
    { return Parsecs; }
    int GetTime()
    { return Time; }
};


// This IRD can dynamically grow to huge sizes
class MegaDog : public Dog
{
    // This member is just so we can remember where we started.
    int InitialSize;
public:
    // Here we see how to express the constructor when we want
    // the code elsewhere. We leave off all references to the
    // base class here, and include it later when we have the
    // actual code.  (See below.)
    MegaDog(char *MegaOwner, int StartSize);
    int Expand()
    {
        // We can't directly access Size, since it's private
        // in the base class "Dog"...
        SetSize (GetSize() * 2);
```

continued on next page

continued from previous page

```
        return GetSize();
    }
    int GetInitial()
    { return InitialSize; }
};

// Here's the actual code for the constructor above.  Remember,
// when we do it this way we need the class name, then the double
// colons ::.  If we forget them, we'll get all kinds of very
// strange errors that are hard to figure out. You might try
// removing the "MegaDog ::" just to see what happens.
MegaDog :: MegaDog(char *MegaOwner, int StartSize) : Dog(MegaOwner, red,
StartSize, "Milk")
{
    // Set the InitialSize to StartSize.
    // This InitialSize attribute is just for remembering
    // where the thing started at.

    InitialSize = StartSize;
}


// This is another generation mutation for use by
// the following two classes.
class CovertDog : public Dog
{
    private:
        int weight;
    protected:
        int stealth;
    public:
        int height;
};

// This is a secret Spy dog
class CIADog : public CovertDog
{
    // All public members of the base class, CovertDog class,
    // are public here, too.  The private members can no longer
    // be seen, but the CIADog can see the protected members
    // of the base class.

    int GetStealth(int which)
    {
        // CIADog class can access the protected members of
        // the base class, and indeed, they're protected members
        // of this class.
        return stealth;
    }
```

```
     int GetHeight(int height)
     {
         // Everyone can see the public members of the base class
         return height;
     }
};

// This is a dog in government protection
class WitnessDog : private CovertDog
{
     // This class can also see the public and protected members
     // of the derived class, as can CIADog, but those members
     // are now all private.  So the outside world can't
     // access them.  That's demonstrated in main.
     public:
         int DaysHiding;
};
```

Listing S4-2 is a main for XDOGS. You can save this file as XDOGS.CPP, and then compile and run it. Be sure to try out some of the suggestions in the code's comments about removing some of the //'s before the lines to see what kinds of errors you get.

Listing S4-2 XDOGS.CPP

```
#include "xdogs.h"
void main()
{
     // Make a flying dog
     FlyingDog jimmy("Jim",10, 100, 1000);
     cout << "Jimmy's flying IRD!" << endl;
     cout << "Traveling at " << jimmy.GetHeight();
     cout << " miles high" << endl;
     cout << "and " << jimmy.GetSpeed() << " miles per hour.";
     cout << endl;

     // Create a warping dog
     WarpingDog JeanLuc("JeanLuc");
     cout << "JeanLuc's dog is starting to warp..." << endl;
     JeanLuc.Start();
     cout << "and first warp coming up..." << endl << endl;
     JeanLuc.DoWarp();
     cout << "New values are " << endl;
     cout << "  Parsecs traveled = " << JeanLuc.GetParsecs();
     cout << endl;
     cout << "  Time traveled = " << JeanLuc.GetTime() << endl;
     cout << "And ready for another warp..." << endl << endl;
```

continued on next page

Sample 4

continued from previous page

```
    JeanLuc.DoWarp();
    cout << "New values are " << endl;
    cout << "  Parsecs traveled = " << JeanLuc.GetParsecs();
    cout << endl;
    cout << "  Time traveled = " << JeanLuc.GetTime();
    cout << endl << endl;

    // Make a MegaDog
    MegaDog Bill("Bill",250);
    cout << "Bill's IRD's starting size is " << Bill.GetSize();
    cout << endl;
    cout << "And he's getting bigger.  Up to " << Bill.Expand();
    cout << endl;
    cout << "And he's getting bigger.  Up to " << Bill.Expand();
    cout << endl;
    cout << "And he's getting bigger.  Up to " << Bill.Expand();
    cout << endl << endl;

    // These next classes just demonstrate what we can access
    // in our program.  Try removing some of the commented stuff
    // described below to see what kinds of errors you get from
    // your compiler.
    // Make a CIA dog
    CIADog george;
    george.height = 10;   // That's public, so we can use it.

    // Remove the double-slashes at the beginning of these next
    // two lines to see the error messages that result.  We
    // can't access those members here!
    // george.weight = 20;   // Private, so we can't see it
    // george.stealth = 99;   // Protected, so we can't see it

    // Make a witness dog
    WitnessDog ron;

    // Here, we can't see any of the members of WitnessDog's base
    // class.  Remove the comments on the next three lines to see
    // the errors.
    // ron.height = 30;
    // ron.weight = 25;
    // ron.stealth = 75;

    // However, we can access the public members in WitnessDog
    ron.DaysHiding = 10000;
}
```

Here's the output for the above program:

```
Jimmy's flying IRD!
Traveling at 100 miles high
and 1000 miles per hour.
JeanLuc's dog is starting to warp...
and first warp coming up...

New values are
Parsecs traveled = 100
Time traveled = 1000
And ready for another warp...

New values are
Parsecs traveled = 200
Time traveled = 2000

Bill's IRD's starting size is 250
And he's getting bigger. Up to 500
And he's getting bigger. Up to 1000
And he's getting bigger. Up to 2000
```

The Real World

The main idea behind inheritance is to create more specialized classes. For example, in a program that keeps track of the inventory at a bookstore, there might be a class called Stock. This would contain attributes that all items in stock possess, such as a price, a description, and an inventory number.

There would be classes derived from Stock, for each of the different types of objects in the bookstore. Some derived classes might be Book, Calendar, and Magazine. Each of these classes would have members specific to that type. For instance, Book might have a Title attribute;

Calendar might have a Year attribute; Magazine might have an Issue attribute, among others.

Then there would be objects belonging to each of these classes. Each specific book would be an object of class Book, and would have the specific attributes filled in, such as Title.

The situation of two copies of the same book could be handled in different ways; one might be to have two objects of class Book, one for each copy.

Another might be to have only one object of class Book for the two books, but have a Copies attribute. Copies would be an integer denoting the number of copies in stock, and will be decreased each time a copy is sold. That way, the people working in the bookstore can check the Copies attribute to see if they have any copies in stock. This number might even be set to 0 when they sell out, and the object would remain on the computer. Then when more come in, the Copies attribute would be updated appropriately.

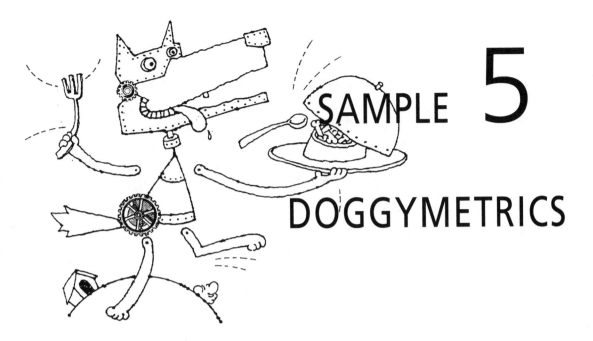

SAMPLE 5

DOGGYMETRICS

We could probably use some way of keeping track of our IRD's exercise, since exercise is vital to the good health of a growing, young IRD.

To do this, we'll create two new classes, one called AerobicDog and one called Exercise.

The AerobicDog is little more than the regular Dog. Notice the constructor has its own defaults, but the first parameter must be specified. Notice also the function DoTuneup. This does little more than call the tuneup function. But...

NEW STUFF: AN OBJECT'S POINTER TO ITSELF

The tuneup function takes as a parameter a pointer to an object of type Dog. When we used this function last time, we just made an object of class Dog and passed its address (using the ampersand, &) to the tuneup function. But how do we specify the address of the current object when we're inside one of the class methods? After all, each class may have several objects belonging to it, so how do we tell the tuneup function (in this case) the address of the current object?

The answer is to use the *this* keyword, as we do in the DoTuneup function. We can only use *this* in a member function, and it's like a variable that always holds the address of the object. So if we have two objects of class AerobicDog, and for each object we call the DoTuneup method, the first time *this* points to the first object; the second time *this* points to the second object.

NEW STUFF: POINTERS TO BASE CLASSES AND DERIVED CLASSES

Notice in the program that we're passing to the tuneup function a *this* pointer, which in this case points to an AerobicDog class. But the tuneup function requires a pointer to a Dog class.

That's okay. That is, it's okay as long as we're passing either a pointer to an actual Dog object or a pointer to an object belonging to a class *derived from* the Dog class.

We can't pass a pointer to an object of a totally separate class, but if the class is derived from the expected class, we're fine, as we are here.

Take a peek at the constructor for the Exercise class. It takes a pointer to an object of class AerobicDog, and the Exercise object stores this pointer in one of its attributes. That means each Exercise object stores a pointer to an AerobicDog object. In other words, we can set up a rather loose association between AerobicDog objects and Exercise objects: For each Exercise object, we have an AerobicDog object.

Notice how in the code for the constructor we save the pointer away for later use. (Remember, it's a pointer to an object, and we can copy that pointer into another pointer variable, in this case, OurDog. That means OurDog still points to the original AerobicDog object. It's a different pointer variable, but it has the address of the same object.)

NEW STUFF: NUMBER CONVERSION AND CASTING

Sometimes we need to do calculations that involve both floating point and decimal. Indeed, in this program we're doing just that when we calculate the average speed. There's really no big problem with this; if the mathematical expression has a float in it, the other numbers are treated as floats, and the final answer is a float.

Sometimes, however, we may have an integer that needs to be passed to a mathematical function requiring a float. The C++ compiler will probably get upset if we try to do that, however, so we have to convert, or *cast*, the integer to a float. The way we do that is to put the new type, float, in parentheses before the variable name.

In the sample below, we demonstrate casting in the main, where we try to pass an integer 10 to the second parameter of the RunMore method, which is expecting a float. We put the word float in parentheses before the number 10.

Listing S5-1 is the header file. Call it EXERCISE.H.

Listing S5-1 EXERCISE.H

```
#include "dog.h"
#include "tuneup.h"

class AerobicDog : public Dog
{
public:
    AerobicDog(char *AerOwner, dogcolors theColor = silver,
        int theSize = 10, char *theFood = "Pizza")
    : Dog(AerOwner, theColor, theSize, theFood)
    {
    }

    //Encapsulation can include the tuneup function
    void DoTuneup()
    { tuneup(this); }
};

class Exercise
{
    AerobicDog *OurDog;
    int Distance;        // How far he's traveled
    float Time;          // How long he's been traveling
    float AverageSpeed;  // Calculated in RunMore method by total
public:
    Exercise (AerobicDog *whichDog)
    {
        OurDog = whichDog;

        // We can't automatically assume the attributes are 0,
        // so we have to initialize them manually.  You might
        // try removing these two lines to see what happens.

        Distance = 0;
        Time = 0;
    }
    void RunMore(int thisDistance, float thisTime)
    {
        int NewSize;
```

continued on next page

continued from previous page

```
        Distance += thisDistance;
        Time += thisTime;

        // Lose some weight
        NewSize = OurDog->GetSize();
        OurDog->SetSize(NewSize - 1);

    }
    float GetAverageSpeed()
    {
        // Speed is in miles per hour, or miles divided by
        // hours... So that's the formula for rate:
        //    Speed = Distance / Time

        return (Distance / Time);
    }
};
```

Listing S5-2 is the main program. Call it whatever you like; perhaps EXERCISE.CPP.

Listing S5-2 EXERCISE.CPP

```
#include "exercise.h"

void main()
{
    AerobicDog Sam("Sam");  // Use the defaults for the
                            // rest of the parameters

    // Now create a new Exercise object.  It needs a pointer
    // to an AerobicDog object...

    Exercise SamRoutine(&Sam);

    // First do a tuneup.  This could also be accomplished
    // by simply
    //      tuneup(&Sam);
    // but it's nice to put it in the class like this.
    Sam.DoTuneup();

    // Dump some data
    cout << "Initial Data" << endl;
    cout << "Size = " << Sam.GetSize() << endl << endl;

    // Do first exercise routine
    SamRoutine.RunMore(10, 5.6);
    cout << "After first exercise..." << endl;
```

```
cout << "Average Speed = " << SamRoutine.GetAverageSpeed();
cout << endl;
cout << "New Size = " << Sam.GetSize() << endl << endl;

// Do second exercise routine
// Notice the casting, as explained in the box above.
SamRoutine.RunMore(20, (float)10);
cout << "After second exercise..." << endl;
cout << "Average Speed = " << SamRoutine.GetAverageSpeed();
cout << endl;
cout << "New Size = " << Sam.GetSize() << endl << endl;
}
```

Compile and run the program. Since we're using the tuneup function, we need to include TUNEUP.CPP in our project, just as we did in Sample 2.

After you run it, the output should look like this:

```
Initial Data
Size = 11


After first exercise...
Average Speed = 1.785714
New Size = 10


After second exercise...
Average Speed = 1.923077
New Size = 9
```

The Real World

In the real world, we often have classes that have attributes that are pointers to other objects. This is one way of building a hierarchy. For example, we might be designing a computer program that keeps track of members of a health club. We might have a Member class, which has all the information on a person: name, address, phone number.

We might also want to keep track of some personal health information, such as the name and address of the person's doctor. Rather than give the entire doctor's name and address in the Member class, we might simply have a second class, called Doctor. This is where the doctor's name and address is stored.

Then, inside the Member class, we would have a pointer to a Doctor object. That way, we can keep the information on the doctors separate, and we don't need to have repeated information if two members happen to go to the same doctor.

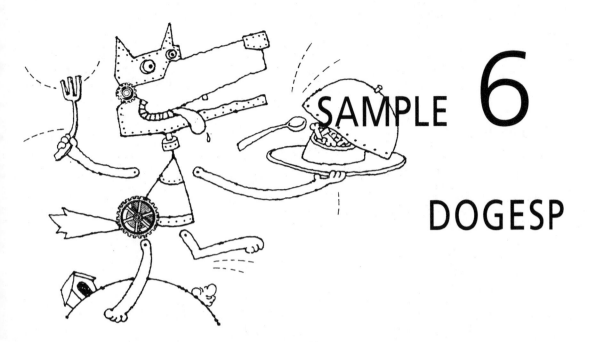

It would probably be nice if the IRD could communicate with other animals over radio waves, sort of like ESP. So perhaps we could have it communicate with the Incredible Robot Cat, which is a secret project happening in the sub-basement of PEts That Think.

We were lucky, because we managed to get hold of some of the code for the Incredible Robot Cats (IRCs). We could probably sell it to the competition for a million dollars and move to the Bahamas, but we don't think that would be very ethical. We'll let our friend Bill do it instead. (Maybe he'll share the money!)

NEW STUFF: FRIENDLY CLASSES

Normally, classes that have private and protected members don't let other classes and functions have access to those members. But every once in a while, there's a good reason that only a certain other class or only a certain function should be granted special access to the private and protected members. These classes and functions are called *friends*. (Really!)

We specify that a class or function is to be a friend by putting the word friend and the class name or function prototype right in our class definition. The code below demonstrates this. Notice the class Cat is a friend to ESPDog, and can directly access the private members of objects of class ESPDog.

Listing S6-1 is a header file demonstrating the friend idea. Type it in and save it as CAT.H. It's used by the next main program, below.

Listing S6-1 CAT.H

```
#include <iostream.h>
#include <string.h>

// The actual Dog class doesn't have Cat as a friend,
// so we'll make a completely new class.
class ESPDog
{
    char name[20];
public:
    ESPDog(char *theName = "NoName")
    {
        strncpy(name, theName, 20);
    }
    void GetName(char *buffer)
    { strncpy (buffer, name, 20); }

    // Cat is a friend, so it can access
    // ESPDog's private members!
    friend class Cat;
};


class Cat
{
    ESPDog *ourFriend;       // Can't just use "friend" since
                             // that's already a word in C++.
    char name[20];
public:
    Cat(char *theName, ESPDog *theFriend)
    {
        strncpy(name, theName, 20);
        ourFriend = theFriend;
    }

    void GetName(char *buffer)
    { strncpy (buffer, name, 20); }

    // Can read friend's private attributes
    void GetFriendName (char *buffer)
    { strncpy (buffer, ourFriend->name, 20); }
};
```

Here's a main program. Save it as SAMP6.CPP, or whatever you like.

```
#include "cat.h"

void main()
{
    ESPDog KidDog("Andrew");       // Use defaults for the rest
                                   // of the parameters
    Cat KidCat("Bill",&KidDog);    // Remember, we need the
                                   // address of KidDog.
    char buffer[20];               // Need this for getting the
                                   // names

    cout << "We have two objects, let's see if they have ESP...";
    cout << endl;
    cout << "They know their own names..." << endl;
    KidDog.GetName(buffer);
    cout << "Dog's name is " << buffer << endl;
    KidCat.GetName(buffer);
    cout << "Cat's name is " << buffer << endl << endl;

    cout << "Does the cat know the dog's name...?" << endl;
    KidCat.GetFriendName(buffer);
    cout << "...it's " << buffer << endl;
}
```

After you compile and run the program, the output should look like this:

We have two objects, let's see if they have ESP...
They know their own names...
Dog's name is Andrew
Cat's name is Bill

Does the cat know the dog's name...?
...it's Andrew

The Real World

Occasionally, you may have two classes that are so closely related they really need to have access to each other's private members. Normally, only public members are accessible by other classes, yet we'd really prefer to keep the members private.

For example, you may have some objects holding data, such as word processor documents. You may then have another object of class Save, whose only purpose is to save these other objects' data to a file.

This Save object would need access to the data in these other objects, so this would be an ideal time for a friend.

One way to think of a friend class is that you're allowing only certain classes (these friend classes) to have access to your data, while the rest of the classes in your program can't touch the data. On the other hand, if you make the data public, then *all* classes can access it.

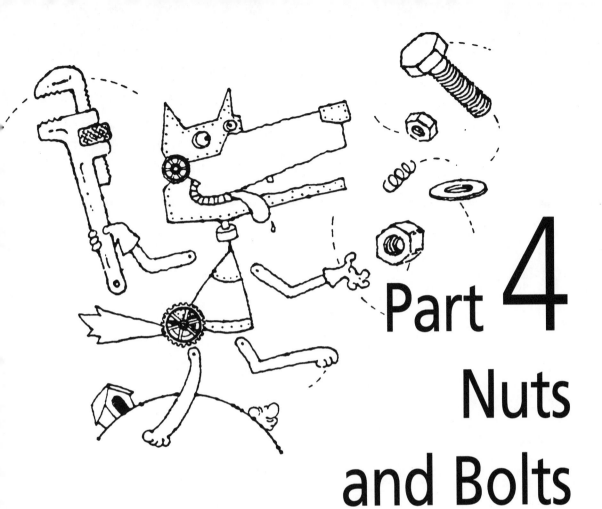

Part 4
Nuts
and Bolts

11
STOP BARKING, IT'S A LIBRARY!

We're still on vacation, but like all programmers, we're still thinking about work. For that matter, we even brought home our copy of the *IRD Programmer's Manual*.

We decide to explore a word we encountered many, many chapters and moons ago.

The word is library.

And that, in fact, is where we are: the public library. It seems our IRD led us here when we asked it what a library is. Makes sense, considering the IRD doesn't talk, and it's also not a programmer. But maybe we can make a connection between the programming term library and a real library.

So what exactly does a real library do? It holds books, and we're free to use any of them.

What is a library in computer terms? It holds either classes or stand-alone functions, and we're free to use any of them.

According to the *IRD Programmer's Manual,* these programming libraries come in all different shapes and sizes, and usually each library contains a set of related class definitions or a set of related functions.

For instance, we've already used the iostream library. This gave us the ability to use cin and cout.

Here's how it works: When we want to use a library, we have to tell the computer we're using it. That's where the #include *directive* comes in.

For instance, consider this small program, Listing 11-1.

Chapter 11

Listing 11-1 Library

```
#include <iostream.h>

void main()
{
    cout << "IRD" << endl;
}
```

This tells the compiler to first read through the file called IOSTREAM.H. Just like everything else in C++, input and output use special objects. These Stream objects are defined in this IOSTREAM.H file. They include Istream and Ostream classes for input and output of a "stream" of data. The cin and cout that we've already been using are objects derived from these two classes. The << and >> operators are actually methods belonging to these classes, and they're overloaded to handle the different data types we've been using, such as int and float.

Other Libraries

As usual, we find we can't bear to go on unless we head home and explore more on the computer. So we leave the public library and go home.

Once home, we fire up the computer. We didn't have a computer before, but the author forgot that fact when he wrote the first sentence in this paragraph. That's allowed, though, because we're living in a book.

So now we have one. It's a pretty nice one, too.

As we dig through the computer, we find that all the files that end with .H, called the *header* files, are all grouped together for us to look at. Here's a small sampling:

- FSTREAM.H
- STRING.H
- MATH.H

We vaguely remember seeing these used in other places in the book . . .

- FSTREAM.H defines some classes for using files.
- STDLIB.H, STRING.H, and MATH.H define some stand-alone functions. For example, STRING.H defines the function

```
char *strcpy(char dest, const char src);
```

which is a function we used before for copying the contents of one string into another.

Table 11-1 lists some more functions and classes defined in these libraries listed above.

Table 11-1 Some functions and classes defined in these libraries

Header File	Description
FSTREAM.H	Defines, among others, the classes Ofstream and Ifstream. We saw in the program samples that these are used for file operations.
STRING.H	Defines several stand-alone functions used for string operations, including the strcpy, strlen, and strcmp routines.
MATH.H	Defines lots of math routines, including functions containing the formulas for a bunch of stuff we may or may not have learned about in school, including sin, cos, and tan.

Another Type

When we peek at the math library, we find that it requires a different type. Most of the math stuff we've done in the past has been using integers and floats. But MATH.H uses something called *double*.

As it turns out, double is very much like float, but can have a lot more digits after the decimal point. Or, it can be a much larger number with not quite as many digits after the decimal. It's a higher *precision* than float.

To use the math routines, we declare variables as double, rather than float. The Program Section at the end of this chapter will have an example.

No Code, and Other Extensions

We're starting to get some questions ready for next week, when we go back to work and see Linda again, but we're not sure we want to wait. So we ask the author to have Linda call us.

Nothing happens.

We tell the author the pizza will be on us the next time we go out.

Nothing.

We clench our teeth and tell the author we like the book a lot, and we ask if we can star in the next one, too.

A noise comes from the IRD's mouth. It's Linda's voice. "Hi! I hear you're exploring class libraries!"

"Yup."

"Great! I'll tell you some more about them, in response to your questions. First, the .H files are known as *header* files. You may have seen that term already, so here's a quick review. The header files have class definitions and function prototypes. We saw function prototypes in the Samples part of the book.

"But," she continues, "what's inside these header files, exactly? Just the definitions and prototypes. The actual code has already been compiled, and is inside what's called the library. This library gets linked into our program after our program is compiled.

"So in other words," she adds, "the header file for the library is read in when the computer encounters an #include directive in our code. The code for the library is linked into our program after our program is compiled."

"Sometimes," she continues, "names of the header files end not with .H, but, rather, with .HPP. That's a new thing with C++. The previous language, C, had code files ending in .C and header files ending in .H. So occasionally people try to be consistent and use the .HPP extension for the header files. But often they just use .H. Most of the libraries that come with the compiler, the ones we saw above, end with just .H. For most compilers, however, the *code* has to end with .CPP. That way the compiler knows whether to compile in C++ or C. If it sees just a .C extension, it knows to just compile in C."

A Word from Our Sponsor

Linda continues. "There are lots of libraries available, and you can order them from software companies. A quick look through a catalog from a mail-order software company shows there are hundreds, maybe even thousands. And remember, the idea behind class libraries is, 'Why should I write the code if someone else already did?'"

"So," we ask, "what do some of these libraries do?"

"They provide all sorts of class libraries and functions. Some make it easier to program graphics, for instance. We'll look at one type in particular in the next chapter. It's for what's called a *windowing system.*"

"So these things are supposed to make life easier?"

"Generally. Take the iostream library, for instance. It makes it easier to display stuff on the screen and to read things from the keyboard."

"Easier than what?"

"Um... Let's suppose you need to display the number stored in an integer variable, and suppose that number is 389. Here's how you would do it. Remember, I'm communicating over the IRD, so I'm transmitting a program right now."

As we watch, a program, Listing 11-2, appears on our computer screen.

Listing 11-2 Library 2

```
#include <iostream.h>
void main()
{
    int somenum;
    somenum = 389;
    cout << somenum << endl;
}
```

We compile and run the program, and see the number 389 appear in the output.

"Let's think about what just happened," says Linda. "The computer first wrote the digit '3', then the digit '8', and then the digit '9'. We then told it to do a newline character. But really, the computer stores the number 389 in its memory as a bunch of electrical signals, and it doesn't store it as three separate digits. It has to figure out which digits the number 389 comprises, and then display them one by one, from left-to-right. Fortunately, though, the iostream library does all that for us! Imagine what a pain in the IRD's behind it would be if we had to write the code to do that!"

We shudder. We don't even want to think about that.

"And that," says Linda, "is what a library is all about. For some more examples, you may want to look back at the Samples section of the book again. Several examples use the fstream library."

The IRD makes a clicking sound as Linda hangs up.

MATH.H Example

We've already seen lots of examples in the past using the libraries FSTREAM.H and STRING.H. So here, we'll look at an example that uses MATH.H.

Recall that we need to use this strange new type called double. Remember, it's just like float, only it can hold more digits per number.

This example uses four functions defined in MATH.H. The first calculates the square root of a number. (In case it's been a while since you've had a math class, when you take a square root of a number, you can multiply the answer by itself to get the original number. So the square root of 25 is 5, since 5 times 5 is 25.)

The second function raises one number to the power of a second. That is, if the first is 3 and the second is 4, it calculates 3 to the 4th power, or 3 * 3 * 3 * 3.

The third and fourth are functions common to computers, which you may not have seen before. They are the *Ceiling* function and the *Floor* function. The Ceiling function takes a number and figures out the next whole number greater than or equal to that number. For example, the ceiling of 3.7 is 4, since 4 is the next whole number greater than 3.7. The ceiling of 5 is 5, since 5 is greater than *or equal to* 5. The ceiling of −3.5 is −3, since −3 is the next whole number greater than or equal to −3.5.

The Floor function is very much like the ceiling function; however, it goes the other direction. It finds whole numbers less than or equal to a number. So the floor of 3.7 is 3; the floor of 5 is 5; and the floor of −3.5 is −4, since −4 is the next whole number less than or equal to −3.5. Table 11-2 shows the MATH.H functions.

Table 11-2 Some functions in MATH.H

Function	What It Does
sqrt	Calculates the square root of a double.
pow	Raises one double to the power of another.
ceil	Finds the whole number greater than or equal to a double.
floor	Finds the whole number less than or equal to a double.

Here's a quick example, Listing 11-3, demonstrating these functions. Notice that even though the Ceiling and Floor functions return a whole number, the type is a double. That just means it always has .0 after it.

Listing 11-3 Library 3

```
#include <iostream.h>
#include <math.h>

void main()
{
    double IRD1size = 3.7;
    double IRD2size = 5.0;
    double IRD3size = -3.5;   // He's upside down.
    double IRD4size = 25;

    // List the sizes

    cout << "The sizes..." << endl;
    cout << IRD1size << endl;
    cout << IRD2size << endl;
    cout << IRD3size << endl;
    cout << IRD4size << endl;
    cout << endl;
```

continued on next page

continued from previous page

```
// Figure the square roots.

cout << "The square roots..." << endl;
cout << "except for #3, since it's negative." << endl;
cout << sqrt(IRD1size) << endl;
cout << sqrt(IRD2size) << endl;
cout << sqrt(IRD4size) << endl;

cout << "Testing the square roots..." << endl;
cout << sqrt(IRD1size) * sqrt(IRD1size) << endl;
cout << sqrt(IRD2size) * sqrt(IRD2size) << endl;
cout << sqrt(IRD4size) * sqrt(IRD4size) << endl;
cout << endl;

// Next, the power of these to 4.
cout << "Raised to the fourth power..." << endl;
cout << pow(IRD1size,4) << endl;
cout << pow(IRD2size,4) << endl;
cout << pow(IRD3size,4) << endl;
cout << pow(IRD4size,4) << endl;
cout << endl;

// The ceiling...
cout << "The ceilings..." << endl;
cout << ceil(IRD1size) << endl;
cout << ceil(IRD2size) << endl;
cout << ceil(IRD3size) << endl;
cout << ceil(IRD4size) << endl;
cout << endl;

// The floor...
cout << "The floors..." << endl;
cout << floor(IRD1size) << endl;
cout << floor(IRD2size) << endl;
cout << floor(IRD3size) << endl;
cout << floor(IRD4size) << endl;
}
```

Notice that when we do the square root section, we have to skip the third size, because square roots of negative numbers are undefined in the usual number system. (You might try including a line to calculate the square root of the third size, just to see how your computer handles the situation.) The output of this program is:

The sizes...
3.7
5
−3.5
25

The square roots...
except for #3, since it's negative.
1.923538
2.236068
5
Testing the square roots...
3.7
5
25

Raised to the fourth power...
187.4161
625
150.0625
390625

The ceilings...
4
5
−3
25

The floors...
3
5
−4
25

Don't Panic

We begin to realize that even though this chapter isn't as long as some of the others, there's a lot of information in it.

We looked at different kinds of libraries. Some provide classes, some provide stand-alone functions.

The iostream and fstream libraries provide classes; the first handles the cout and cin stuff, among other things, and the second handles file operations.

The string and math libraries provide stand-alone functions for handling (no surprise) string and math functions. Cool, huh?

We nod in agreement to humor the author.

12
AS THE IRD LOOKS OUT THE WINDOW

As we play with the new computer the author gave us in the last chapter, we're finding some cool stuff about it.

First, it's got a really good computer version of solitaire, where you play against the computer. If you win, the screen shows a great animated sequence of 100 decks of cards being dropped out of an airplane over Seattle. The cards get scattered all over both the city and the computer screen.

But there's another piece of software that came with the computer: a windowing system. To find out just what a windowing system is, we decide to call Linda.

Unfortunately, somebody knocks at the door before we have a chance to call. We go over to the door and open it. It's Bill!

"Bill!" What do you say to a guy with the nerve to come around after brazenly ripping you off? Well, since we know he's just here to help explain programming windowing systems, we decide to play it cool. "Come on in! You're just the guy I was looking for."

"Oh yeah?" He's looking edgy, like he might be thinking twice about being here. Then he notices our new computer with a gleam of horrified recognition in his eyes. "Hey, you double dealing sneak! That's mine! I stole it fair and square!"

We change the subject. "We heard this computer has a windowing system. Could you show us what it is and how it operates?"

Chapter 12

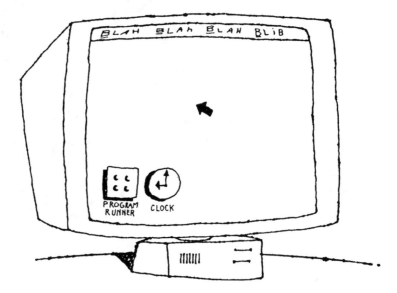

Figure 12-1 The windowing system

"Oh, um, okay. This particular machine is set up so that you simply type 'w' and press the enter key to start the windowing system."

"Is that true for all computers?"

"No. For many computers, the windowing system comes up automatically when you turn on the computer. For other computers, like this one, you have to type something, usually either 'w' or 'win' or something like that."

We type 'w' and press return, and the pictures on the screen change. The whole background is blue, and there are a couple of tiny little pictures in the lower left-hand corner of the screen. One looks like a little clock, and it has the correct time. Underneath the little clock is the word, "Clock." The other little picture is just a rectangle with some little marks inside it. The little marks are too small to see what they are. Under this little rectangle are the words, "Program Runner."

There's also a little arrow in the middle of the screen. The screen looks like Figure 12-1.

Bill points to the little clock. "Double-click on that icon."

"Excuse me?"

"Move the mouse so the little arrow points to the little clock, and click the button on the mouse twice."

We do so, and the clock grows in size, until it's about one-quarter the size of the screen. It's surrounded by some strange symbols, and looks like Figure 12-2.

"This rectangular thing the clock's inside of," explains Bill, "is called a window. Right now there's only one window, but when we run other programs, more windows appear. Each window holds some information. We can move the window around and change its size using the mouse. To move the window, position the little arrow over the bar with the title 'Clock' inside it."

We do so.

"Now press the button and don't let go. Move the mouse."

As we move the mouse with the button pressed, the window moves with the little arrow.

"Now let go."

We let go of the button and the window stays in its new position.

"Next, position the pointer carefully over the border."

We position the arrow over the right edge of the window, and when we get it positioned, the arrow turns into a small horizontal line with arrowheads on both ends.

"Press the button and, holding it down, move the mouse again."

Figure 12-2 The clock screen

We do so. As we move the pointer to the right, the clock grows in size on the right side.

"You can also make it get taller or shorter or thinner or whatever, by doing that to the different edges," says Bill. "Now look at the two buttons in the upper right-hand corner. The left one has an arrowhead pointing down, the right one has an arrowhead pointing up. Click the one on the right, with the up-arrow."

We do it, and the window grows until it's filling the entire screen.

"We just maximized the window," says Bill. "Click again on the same button you just did."

We do it again, and the window reverts to its previous size and position.

"Now click the other one, the one with the down-arrow."

We click it, and the clock gets small again, back to a little icon in the lower left-hand corner of the screen.

"You just minimized the window," says Bill.

Bill then points to the little button in the upper left-hand corner of the screen. "Don't do it right now," he says, "but clicking on that button will close the window and shut down that particular program. We'll try it later."

So What Good Is the Windowing System?

Bill reads the section header, and answers the question. "Actually, the windowing system provides the *graphical user interface,* or GUI—that is, it provides a set of interface units for different programs. Remember, you learned about interface units back in Chapter 7. The window containing the clock is the interface unit for the objects in the clock program."

He continues, "There can be a number of programs running at once, each with its own window. And when their windows are minimized to an icon, the programs are still running, but we can't do much with them until we open the windows back up."

A Buncha Interface Units

Bill points to the little icon with the words Program Runner under it. "Double-click on that."

We do so, and it grows into another window. It looks like Figure 12-3.

There are little pictures inside it. They have underneath them names such as Salaries, Word Processor, and Visual Cobol.

Figure 12-3 The Program Runner screen

"Those little pictures," says Bill, "are icons, just as the little things in the lower left-hand corner are also icons. These icons, however, don't represent minimized windows for programs running. Rather, they represent programs that are available for us to start running. That's why this program and its window are both called Program Runner. Other systems have programs like Program Runner, but they may have other names."

We ask what the little icons represent.

"The one called Salaries is some sample data to play with. Sort of demonstrates the computer. The one called Visual Cobol is a brand new, state of the art program development system for the language called Cobol. That's a language we don't really care about where we work, though. It's mainly used for things like accounting and what-not. The Word Processor is for typing papers and things." He points to the one called Salaries. "Double-click on that."

We double-click it, Program Runner minimizes, and a new window appears, with the word "Salaries" across the top. Inside the window is a list with two columns headed Name and Salary. Under the Name heading is a list of all the employees of PETT, and their salaries are under the Salary heading. Where on earth did Bill get this program from?

Bill suddenly gets very nervous. "Oops, that's the wrong, um . . ." He grabs the mouse and double-clicks in the upper left-hand corner, closing

Figure 12-4 The Sample Data screen

the window. He's shaking, and talking really fast. "Um, that was just some sample stuff I put on the computer last week after I bought it . . . Um . . . I didn't steal the data from work, it was, um given to me by that guy in accounting . . . er, um . . . I mean he just . . ."

He stops dead silent and is wide eyed. He's sweating madly. Slowly and deliberately, he says, "Pull up Program Runner again." His voice is cracking.

We do so.

"Double-click on that icon that has the words Sample Data under it."

We do it, and once again Program Runner minimizes and a new window forms. This window has a title bar across the top, like the others, but its title is Sample Data. Inside the window are some words and little squares, as in Figure 12-4.

Behind the Window

"Remember," says Bill, "that each window corresponds to a program that's running. All these programs run at the same time, and each program must tell the windowing system to make a new window, and the program must describe what the window looks like. The program must then tell the windowing system what buttons and things to put inside the window.

"So how," he continues, "do we programmers write programs to run under these windowing systems? Well, first we generally use a class library. These class libraries provide object classes corresponding to the different interface units—the windows, the buttons, etc. When we want to make a new window, we make a new object of class Window—or whatever name the particular library uses for the class. Then the computer makes for us a simulated memory object inside the computer's memory, which simulates the behavior of the window. We also get an actual interface unit, the window itself.

"But," he adds, "we need more. We need to write the code for the methods that get activated in response to things happening to the window. When our program is running, for instance, and we click the Close button, we might have a method that gets activated which displays a little message on the screen asking the user if he or she really wants to close the window.

"In fact," he says, "this Sample Data program has that feature. Click the little button in the upper left-hand corner of the screen."

We do so, and a message appears in its own little window, as in Figure 12-5.

Figure 12-5 Sample Data asks a question

"Click the No button," says Bill.

We do it.

"Now," says Bill, "let's think about what the programmers did when they wrote this part of the program. They created a new object of class Window, and they included a method that gets activated when the Close button is clicked.

"In that method," he says, "the programmers have written the code for creating a new object of class 'message,' or whatever class name the library uses. The programmer included in the constructor for this Message object the text to appear in the message. In this case, it was 'Are you sure you want to close SAMPLE DATA?' After that, the computer created the message box, and the user selected one of the buttons.

"Our Close method then checks one of the attributes of this Message object, probably called the Response attribute. If the Response has a 'yes' in it, it means the user selected the Yes button, and our close method can tell the windowing system to close the window and end our program.

"If, on the other hand, the Message object's Response attribute had a 'no' in it, our Close method should just finish without closing the sample program."

"Let's write that in semi-English," he says. He runs out to his car and returns with a chalkboard. He sets it on the couch, dumping chalk dust all over everything. He writes:

```
class window
method: CloseButtonPressed
    Make a new Message Object
    If message object's Response attribute is 'yes'
        ask windowing system to close our window
```

"And when the windowing system closes our window," says Bill, "it also ends our program. And that's it!"

Know When to Open, Know When to Close

"There's one more issue we need to think about," says Bill. "And that's the problem of getting our objects behaving at the same time as our interface units. In particular, when our program creates a new Window

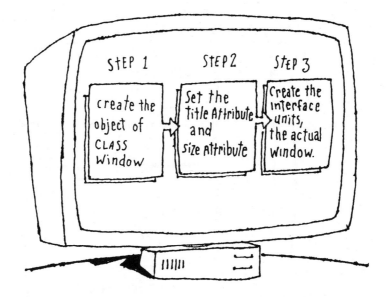

Figure 12-6 Creating windows

object, should the windowing system immediately make the window? It seems so, but what if there are attributes in the class that we need to first set, before the actual window can be created? You know, attributes like how big to make the window, what words should be in the title bar, and so on. That means we need to make an object of this class, then set the attributes. And only *then* can we finally make the window. So it seems we don't want to create the actual window until after we've made an object and set some of its attributes. Figure 12-6 shows what I mean!"

"And how," he continues, "do we perform these steps? Different libraries use different approaches. Most require us to first create a new object of class Window, or whatever name the library uses. Then we call methods for setting the title and size. And only then can we finally call a Create method, which actually creates the window itself."

"Wait a minute," we say. "Are we writing these methods, or are they already in the class library?"

"Excellent question! Normally, Window is a base class containing methods such as Create, which already has the code to create the interface unit. We then derive a new class, say MyWindow, from the class Window. That means our new class gets all these same methods, including the Create

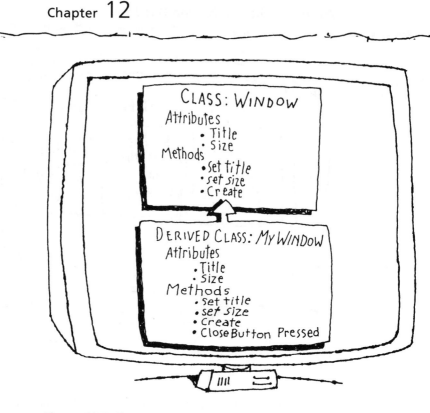

Figure 12-7 CloseButtonPressed method

method. But we can add new methods, such as the CloseButtonPressed method we saw a few paragraphs back. Figure 12-7 has an example."

We look around the room until we first spot the CloseButtonPressed method a few paragraphs back, and then we spot Figure 12-7.

"The code," says Bill, "for the SetTitle, SetSize, and Create methods is already in the library. When we derived our new class, MyWindow, we inherited those methods. But we need to add the CloseButtonPressed method, which does the stuff about asking the users if they really want to close the window.

"Really," he adds, "there would probably already be a CloseButton-Pressed method in the base class Window, which might close the window without asking for permission. Then we would be redefining the Close method in our derived class, MyWindow."

Don't Panic

Bill quickly reminds us not to panic, because the stuff really isn't that bad. "You may feel a little overwhelmed," he says, "but don't worry if you do. If you don't feel overwhelmed, I commend you. Either way, you've done well in getting this far." He pauses. "Have I heard this somewhere before? Oh well, let's glance at what we've covered. And remember, we can always review it or even reread it. Even the greatest programmers don't catch on to everything instantly! Here's what we covered:

- "Windowing systems give us nice little windows to hold our data, and these windows can be opened and closed, moved around, and resized.

- "We use class libraries to program these windows, and we make new objects belonging to these classes. The methods in these objects, then, create the actual window interface units.

- "There's a definite order to the way window objects and subsequently window interface units are created.

- "We can derive new classes from the base window class to add new methods, and these methods tell the computer how to respond to things like when the user clicks the Close button."

Bill looks at his watch and says, "Well, I must be moving on. I'll send you a bill for my time. Well, actually, I'll just put it on your credit card. Bye!"

He's out the door in a flash.

13

SOME NUTS AND BOLTS

Our vacation is nearly done, and we decide to spend the next two chapters finishing up our studies of C++, and filling in the gaps with anything left out. Because of this, we decide we'd better keep the chapters short. After all, we're about ready to call it a day and say, "I know C++!"

We've stumbled across a rather startling point; it seems we're actually starting to understand the *IRD Programmer's Manual*. In some ways, that's kind of scary, but it's probably to be expected, since most computer texts assume you already have a strong knowledge of the subject, and this is no exception. We can only conclude that by now we've already got a pretty strong knowledge of C++!

So for this chapter and the next, we'll see if we can get away with not calling on the help of our co-workers. It'll be just us, our IRD, our computer, and the *IRD Programmer's Manual*.

Pounding Out Some #'s

The first thing we decide to explore today is that somewhat mysterious #include statement.

The *IRD Programmer's Manual* tells us that when the computer compiles a program, it watches for the lines beginning with a pound sign, #, and these lines tell the compiler how to behave.

For instance, if the compiler encounters the line

```
#include <iostream.h>
```

it knows to read through the file called IOSTREAM.H before compiling the rest of the program.

It turns out there are actually other statements we can have that begin with the # sign. Because the compiler watches for these first, the computer people have said the compiler processes these lines first, or preprocesses them. So they are called *preprocessor* statements.

There are several other preprocessor statements, but we don't care about most of them. However, a couple of them are rather important. To demonstrate these, we'll actually use a program. We type in Listing 13-1.

Listing 13-1 Preprocessor

```
#include <iostream.h>

#define DEBUG

int DoMath (int start)
{

// This allows us to watch what value is going
// into DoMath and fix any bugs.

#ifdef DEBUG
    cout << "***DoMath received" << start << endl;
#endif

    start = (start + 8) / 2;
    return start;
}

void main()
{
    int entry;

    cout << "Enter a number" << endl;
    cin >> entry;

    entry += 5;
    cout << "The number plus 5 is" << endl;
    cout << entry << endl;

    cout << "The number plus 8 and divided by two is" << endl;
    cout << DoMath(entry) << endl;
}
```

When we compile and run this program, we see the following output. (We enter 10 in response to the prompt "Enter a number".)

```
Enter a number
10
The number plus 5 is
15
The number plus 8 and divided by two is
***DoMath received 15
11
```

Before we look at what exactly the preprocessor statements in this program do, remove the line

`#define DEBUG`

Then recompile and run the program. The output should look like this:

```
Enter a number
10
The number plus 5 is
15
The number plus 8 and divided by two is
11
```

Notice what's happening. In the second version of the program, the cout line in the DoMath function didn't get compiled. It's not that the program simply didn't do those lines; rather, those lines were actually *skipped* by the compiler in exactly the same way comment // lines are. That means we're telling the compiler to include or exclude certain parts of our program when we compile it. Here's how it works:

The line

`#define DEBUG`

tells the compiler to remember the word DEBUG, but only while it's compiling. Then, later, the lines

`#ifdef DEBUG`

`#endif`

tell the compiler that if DEBUG is defined, compile the statements in between these two lines. But if DEBUG *isn't* defined, simply skip those lines, in the same way the compiler skips comments.

(By the way, note that #ifdef is pronounced either "if defined," or "if-def.")

It's important to realize that DEBUG is not a variable in our program. It's only used by the compiler to include or exclude lines in our program when it compiles it. This is known as a *conditional compile*.

But why would we do that?

Because when we're developing a program, we may have mistakes in it. These mistakes are called "bugs"; and when we're working on fixing the bugs, we're "debugging" the program.

Often when we debug a program, we need to have the program do certain things, such as print the values of certain variables. But we don't want it to do those things when the program is finished and ready to be used by other people. And that's where conditional compile comes in.

We could just remove some of the cout lines, but this way is better, because later, if a person using our program calls us up and says he or she found an error, we can put the

```
#define DEBUG
```

back in our program, and recompile it, without having to retype all the cout lines. We can figure out what's going on, fix it, and then remove the #define DEBUG and recompile it. Then we can send the revised version of the program to our user.

So we hear from a user that there's an error in our program. She entered in a 10, and it told her that 10+5 is 15, which is correct. Then it told her that when she adds 8 to 10, then divides by 2, the answer's 11. But that's not correct: (10+8)/2 is 9.

Of course, we can probably figure out why this is happening, but in larger programs, it's usually not that easy. So let's look at the debug output. (That's the output from the first version of the program, above.)

We see in the debug output that DoMath received the number 15. But that's wrong. It should have received a 10. And why did it receive 15? Because we added 5 to our input value of 10, to make 15. Really, in our main, we only want to print out what 5 more than our value is, but not actually change our value. So we remove the statement

```
entry += 5
```

and change two statements later from

```
cout << entry << endl;
```

to

```
cout << entry + 5 << endl;
```

We then remove the #define DEBUG line (if it's there), and the program now looks like Listing 13-2:

Listing 13-2 Preprocessor 2

```
#include <iostream.h>

int DoMath (int start)
{

// This allows us to watch what value is going
// into DoMath and fix any bugs.

#ifdef DEBUG
    cout << "***DoMath received" << start << endl;
#endif


    start = (start + 8) / 2;
    return start;
}
```

continued on next page

continued from previous page

```
void main()
{
    int entry;

    cout << "Enter a number" << endl;
    cin >> entry;

    cout << "The number plus 5 is" << endl;
    cout << entry + 5 << endl;

    cout << "The number plus 8 and divided by two is" << endl;
    cout << DoMath(entry) << endl;
}
```

We run the program, and the output looks like this, which is correct.

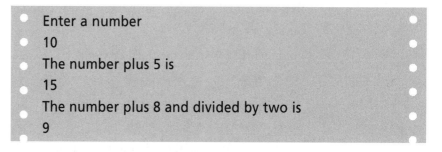

```
Enter a number
10
The number plus 5 is
15
The number plus 8 and divided by two is
9
```

Including an Include File

We recall in the sample programs, when we wrote our own header file containing some class definitions, we included this header file at the beginning of most of our programs.

As we're reading the *Manual*, we stumble across an interesting phenomenon in regard to including files. Take a peek at Listing 13-3. (Warning: When you type in and compile this program, you will probably get some error messages. That's okay, because you're supposed to.) We type this in and save it as HEADER1.H.

Listing 13-3 HEADER1.H

```
class FirstIRD
{
public:
    int FirstID;
};
```

Second, we type in Listing 13-4 and save it as HEADER2.H.

Listing 13-4 HEADER2.H

```
#include "HEADER1.H"
class SecondIRD
{
public:
        FirstIRD MyFirst;  // because of this line, we need HEADER1.H
        int AnotherID;
};
```

Finally, we type in Listing 13-5 for the main, save it as 13-5.CPP and compile it.

Listing 13-5 13-5.CPP

```
#include <iostream.h>
#include "HEADER1.H"
#include "HEADER2.H"

void main()
{
    FirstIRD theOne;
    SecondIRD theTwo;

    // Fill in the only ID for theOne
    theOne.FirstID = 10;

    // Fill in the two IDs for theTwo
    theTwo.AnotherID = 20;
    theTwo.MyFirst.FirstID = 30;

    // C-out the stuff
    cout << "The first has ID " << theOne.FirstID << endl;
    cout << "The second has IDs ";
    cout << theTwo.AnotherID << " & " << theTwo.MyFirst.FirstID << endl;
}
```

Notice the HEADER2.H file includes HEADER1.H. But notice our main program file also includes HEADER1.H before including HEADER2.H. This will cause a problem, because the compiler will first encounter the line #include HEADER1.H, and read through HEADER1.H. Next it will read through HEADER2.H, and get to a second occurrence of #include HEADER1.H. So it will once again read through HEADER1.H, and get an error. Why? Because it can only define any class once, and by reading through HEADER1.H a second time, it tries to define the class FirstIRD a second time.

So how do we fix that? We pull out the *Manual* and find another example. We type Listing 13-6. It's really Listing 13-2, slightly modified.

Listing 13-6 HEADER3.H

```
#ifndef HEADER1
#define HEADER1

class FirstIRD
{
public:
      int FirstID;
};

#endif
```

We notice the first include file starts with,

```
#ifndef HEADER1
```

and ends with

```
#endif
```

which means "If HEADER1 is *not* defined, do all this stuff up until the #endif." So in other words, if HEADER1 is not defined, go through the class definitions.

But why would HEADER1 be defined? And how does it get defined? It gets defined by a

```
#define HEADER1
```

But that never happened!

Exactly!

So the computer does the class definitions. But before it does, it encounters

```
#define HEADER1
```

and so HEADER1 *is now defined*. Which means that the next time we try to include this file, HEADER1 is defined. So when it encounters the line

```
#ifndef HEADER1
```

it will say, "If HEADER1 is not defined, do this stuff. But HEADER1 *is* defined, so don't do this stuff and skip right to the #endif."

Gosh. That's pretty twisted. Let's look at it again.

The first time through, HEADER1 is not defined, so define HEADER1 and do the class definitions.

The second time through, HEADER1 is defined, so don't do the class definitions.

So the stuff in the HEADER1 file is used once—and only once.

Now it's starting to make sense. We look at the program again and think about it. And by golly, we're following it!

We run the program. This time it compiles okay, and has the following output:

> The first has ID 10
> The second has IDs 20 & 30

The Final Word on Program Format

Way back at the beginning, we were concerned about when to use semicolons and how to format our programs in general.

First, the Final Words on Semicolons. Here they are:

FINAL WORDS ON SEMICOLONS

1. Semicolons go at the end of a class definition, after the closing curly bracket, }.

2. Every statement must have a semicolon after it, but a curly bracket never needs a semicolon after it, except in the case of class definitions and structures (we'll come to that in Chapter 14).

Second, some notes on formatting and code design in general.

CODE DESIGN

Rule #1: Nobody agrees on the precise interpretation of these rules, so take them with a grain of salt.

Rule #2: Make your code readable. Everybody considers their own code readable, so do the best you can. Rules #3 and #4 expand on this.

Rule #3: Use names that make sense. Instead of variables like X, Y, and RESULT, use names like BankBalance or Distance or whatever.

continued on next page

continued from previous page

Rule #4: Use lots of indenting and white space.

Rule #5: Be consistent. If you use one form of indenting in your code, use it in the rest of the code. Don't change within a single program. You should probably even be consistent between all your programs, but that probably won't happen as you gradually decide on new approaches.

Rule #6: Use lots of comments beginning with //'s. As annoying as they may be, they really are important. A good exercise to prove this to yourself is to write as long of a program as you can, and don't include a single comment. Then put it down and come back to it a month later. See if you can follow it.

Rule #7: Don't be defensive of your code. There's always a better way. Keep exploring!

If you can abide by these rules, not only will you be a good programmer, you will be a programmer liked by other people. But remember, everybody uses different rules for formatting, so be ready. Take an If statement, for instance:

```
if (finished==1)
{
    cout << "done!" << endl;
        cout << "really!" << endl;
}
```

Some people would prefer this to be typed as

```
if (finished==1) {
    cout << "done!" << endl;
        cout << "really!" << endl;
}
```

(The idea is that with 1,000 If statements in a single program, that's 1,000 fewer lines of code.) So do the best you can and be consistent.

That's enough for this chapter.

14
IF YOU'RE CURIOUS ABOUT C

Well, we've finally made it to the last chapter. Whew!

And we still have a couple of questions.

They're regarding that old language C++ came from, called C. Really, we only have one question: What's the difference?

We ask the *IRD Programmer's Manual*, and find an interesting point. It seems our C++ compiler can also compile C programs. In fact, almost everything you can do in C you can also do in C++. That's because C++ is sort of a "bigger" C. The inventors of C++ took C and added on to it. So all the old stuff about C, both good and bad, is still left over in C++.

No Class

Here's one thing about C: It has no class. It doesn't allow classes. Which means it can't create objects as we know them.

Instead, it has something called a *structure*, which we can also use in C++, and indeed, may want to from time to time.

A structure is sort of like a class with no members, only attributes, and they're all public. So there are no public, private, and protected words inside it. That's all. Listing 14-1 demonstrates structures.

Chapter 14

Listing 14-1 Structure Example

```
#include <iostream.h>

struct NoClass
{
    int onlyAttrib;
    int NoPrivate;
};

void main()
{
    struct NoClass NoObject;
    NoObject.onlyAttrib = 1;
    NoObject.NoPrivate = 2;

    cout << NoObject.onlyAttrib << " ";
    cout << NoObject.NoPrivate << endl;

}
```

The output for this program is just

1 2

Notice in the main, when we declare NoObject as a NoClass structure, we need to begin the declaration with the word struct. That's just a little annoyance about C.

To access the members of the structure, we do it just as we did with objects. Use a period "." to access the members of an object; use a "->" to access the members of an object we're pointing to.

No cout Thang

The cin and cout objects are new to C++. So what did that mean for C? It meant C had a totally different way to do input and output.

Since this isn't a book on C, we won't give all the details here. But it might be good to peek at it, just so we know it's there. Take a look at Listing 14-2.

Listing 14-2 Structure Example 2

```
#include <stdio.h>

void main()
{
    int Annoying, Worse;
    int Boring, NoNeck;

    Annoying = 10;
    Worse = 20;

    printf ("Annoying = %d and Worse = %d\n", Annoying, Worse);
    printf ("Please enter in a value for Boring\n");
    printf ("and then a value for NoNeck, pressing return\n");
    printf ("after each.\n");

    scanf ("%d\n%d", &Boring, &NoNeck);
    printf ("Boring = %d and NoNeck = %d\n", Boring, NoNeck);
}
```

Notice the new header file, STDIO.H. This is what C used instead of IOSTREAM.H. This gave function prototypes for some input/output functions, specifically printf and scanf. printf (pronounced "print-eff") is for printing stuff on the screen; scanf (pronounced "scan-eff") is for reading stuff from the keyboard.

As parameters, printf takes a string for starters, followed by the variables to be printed. The string tells the computer how to format the variables being printed. It's a rather strange approach, but inside the format string are a bunch of % symbols. These correspond to the variables that follow. Following each % is a letter denoting the type of respective variable. (C wasn't quite smart enough to know that since A is an integer, it's still an integer in the printf function. So we had to explicitly tell it inside the format string.)

Notice the \n inside the quotes. This is just like the endl when we're using cout. That is, it causes a so-called newline character to be printed.

A good way to think of the printf is that it prints the format string, but replaces the %'s with the respective variables in the list that follows. So in the above example,

```
printf ("Annoying = %d and Worse = %d\n", Annoying, Worse);
```

tells the computer to replace the first %d with the value for Annoying, and the second %d with the value for Worse. So if Annoying is 10, and Worse is 20, this line would result in this:

> Annoying = 10 and Worse = 20

And scanf works in a similar way; the format string tells what order the things will be typed in; the variables that follow are the variables that we're filling with values.

So the output for the above program, assuming we entered the values 30 and 40 when requested, looks like this:

> Annoying = 10 and Worse = 20
> Please enter in a value for Boring
> and then a value for NoNeck, pressing return
> after each.
> 30
> 40
> Boring = 30 and NoNeck = 40

But there's something highly annoying about scanf. It requires the addresses of the variables, not the variables themselves. That's why all the &'s in Listing 14-2.

But there's something even more annoying. Outrageously annoying, actually. If you use scanf much (not that you should, since cin works better), you will forget these &'s on occasion, and the compiler will not give you an error. Your program simply won't run right, that's all. The reason is that all variables are ultimately stored in the computer in the form of numbers, and the computer reads those numbers and assumes they are the address of some variable. And when you type in the information in response to a scanf statement, it saves the data in some nonexistent variable in never-never land. The first result? A program that doesn't behave in any way like it's intended. The second result? High blood pressure, possibly accompanied by a computer that's been thrown out of the window.

After some contemplation, we decide cin is the better choice, and we only need to know about scanf in the event that someone else used it, and we need to read their code.

That's all.

Call it a day.

No, better yet, call it a language! We're done! Turn the page for a really cool author's note!

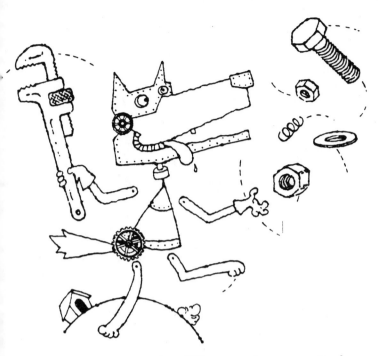

FINAL WORD

Our IRD enters the room, sits down, and sentimentally looks us in the eye. We then begin to think about how it's been a long haul, but we finally made it! And through the course of the book, we actually picked up a little (maybe even alot!) about C++, object-oriented programming, and event-driven programming!

The author finally comes forward, shakes our hand, and says, "I couldn't have done it without you, kind reader. I appreciate your help. I would include your name in the Acknowledgments section, but you have too many names! And thanks for tolerating my use of the non-word 'alot' in the previous paragraph. I've always wanted to put that in print. And more importantly, thanks for reading! I hope it's been fun!"

He hops onto his brand new custom-built Incredible Robot Horse named Metal, and rides off into the sunset.

We turn off the computer, sit down next to our IRD, and finish eating our pizza.

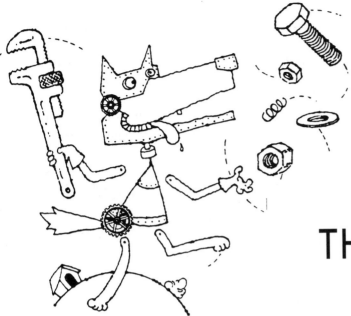

EPILOGUE: RETOOLING THE FACTORY

Since this book used a rather unusual example throughout it—Incredible Robot Dogs—it might not hurt to have one final glance at a more realistic example. So let's retool the factory to create something more practical: a checkbook. Without looking at any code, let's see if we can briefly think about what objects go into a checkbook program.

First, we would need the actual Checkbook object. This has attributes consisting of other objects, such as the check register object, and several check objects, usually 25.

Then we would need the methods. What are the abilities of the objects above?

The checkbook has the ability to have a check torn out of it, and it has the ability to have its checks replaced when they run out. This means it needs to keep track of which check we're on, and seeing if it's the last in the book. So that, in turn, means we need two more attributes for the checkbook object: current check number, and last check number in this book.

The Check Register object has the ability to store several transactions. It also has the ability to have its balance increased and decreased. (This means it needs a few attributes: a balance, and several transactions. Fortunately, most check registers only hold a limited number of transactions, and when those are full, we replace the register with a blank one, carrying forward the balance.)

Then there's the check object: Each check has a number. As we write a check, we fill in a person or company's name, an amount, a date, and possibly a memo. There's also some stuff common to all checks: our own name, address, and other information about us, and our signature. We probably wouldn't want our signature stored on computer, though, since it would be too easy for people to copy.

After we write a check, the information is passed on to the check register, where it's recorded. The check is torn out, and the check number is increased.

So let's summarize:

1. First, the Checkbook class:

    Attributes: Check register
    First Check in book
    Second Check in book
    Third Check in book . . . and so on. This could be an array.
    Current Check Number
    Last Check in this book

    Methods: Tear Out Check. Adds one to the check number.
    Replace Checks

2. Next, the Check Register class:

    Attributes: Balance
    Transactions. Probably an array

    Methods: Deposit. This means increase the balance.
    Withdraw. This means decrease the balance.
    New Register. This will clear the transactions (or save them to disk)

3. And finally, the Check class:

    Attributes: Number
    Who It's To
    Amount
    Date
    Memo
    Our Name
    Our Address

Methods: Write Check. Calls check register's Withdraw method. Also calls checkbook's Tear Out Check method.

The next steps would be to decide what's public and what's private. Notice no classes call the Replace Checks method in Checkbook, so this would probably be private, and called by Checkbook's own Tear Out Check method when the checks are all gone.

And what about constructors and destructors?

The Checkbook constructor would probably take as a parameter a starting check number and a starting balance. This constructor would then create all the checks in the book (probably 25 of them) along with the initial check register object.

Each check that gets created would need to know its number, so that would be a parameter in the check constructor. The check register would need its initial balance, so that would be its constructor's parameter.

And you're welcome to take it from here!

GLOSSARY

Attribute: A piece of data associated with a class. It can be a number, a string of characters, an enum, or another object. The actual value can be different for each object in the class.

Class: A kind or type of object. Can be used for grouping objects together. Every object must belong to a class.

Command: A word that tells the computer to do something. Generally, it's a verb.

Computerized media: A place where computer information is stored and remembered after the computer is turned off. Examples are floppy disks, CD-ROMs, and fixed (or hard) disks.

DogESP (DOG-ee-es-pee) (n) A skill where an Incredible Robot Dog can exchange thoughts with a friendly cat.

Doggycology (DOG-ee-cowl-eh-gee) (n) The study of food being processed by an Incredible Robot Dog.

Doggynetices (DOG-ee-NET-iks) (n) The study of an Incredible Robot Dog's exercise.

Doggynitialize (DOG-ee-NISH-el-ize) (v) The act of initializing an Incredible Robot Dog.

Doggypieces (DOG-ee-pee-siz) (n) The things left behind when a dog's information is saved to some form of computerized media, such as a hard disk.

Doggytuneup (DOG-ee-Tune-up) (v) The act of tuning up an Incredible Robot Dog's levels.

Dogmutations (DOG-myew-TAY-shuns) (n) The act of mutating (i.e., changing the genetic makeup) of an Incredible Robot Dog.

Event-driven programming: The part of programming where associations are made between interface units and methods. Then user actions trigger the appropriate methods.

Function: A piece of a program that performs a task. It may take one or more parameters, and may return something. A method is an example of a function.

Interface Unit: The thing through which a simulated memory object communicates with the real world. This interface unit could simply be an image on the computer screen, such as a button.

Member: A generic term for any attribute or method. The attributes and methods are all members of the class.

Method: An ability an object possesses. In computers, this exists as a function that sits inside a class.

Object: Anything. Any thing that we can conceive is an object. When we're dealing with computers, we can simulate such objects, and this simulated memory object existing inside the computer memory is often simply referred to as the object.

Object-oriented programming: The method of programming where the programmer concentrates on the objects being modeled, and writes code consisting of classes of these objects, including attributes and methods.

Parameter: A word following a command giving more information. Sort of like using a direct object in the English language.

Private: A member that can only be accessed by the methods inside the class.

Protected: A member that can only be accessed by the methods inside the class, and the methods inside the derived classes.

Public: A member that can be accessed by any other class. The public methods serve as the communication device by the class; it's through these public methods that the other parts of the program can access the class.

Simulated memory object: The code inside the *computer program* that models the real-world object. Usually exists as an object of a certain class.

Statement: A complete sentence for the computer. Tells the computer to do one particular task.

FOR FURTHER READING

A short stroll through a large bookstore will show you there are hundreds, maybe even thousands of computer books. Then, there are lots and lots on C and C++ alone, and several on Object-Oriented Programming.

If you want to further your exploration, here are just a few that might help.

C++ for Programmers (Benjamin/Cummings, 1989). This book is clearly written and is a good path for people who know some C to work their way into C++.

Object Oriented Programming: An Introduction, Greg Voss. (McGraw Hill, 1992). An excellent book, but a tad heavy for beginners. Possibly a good book to read after mastering Simple C++. It's thorough, very well-written and easy-to-read.

The Waite Group's C Programming Using Turbo C++, 2nd ed. (SAMS, 1993). Teaches C++ with one of the most popular C++ compilers for the PC, including PC graphics functions.

The Waite Group's C++ Primer Plus (Waite Group Press, 1991). Another good C++ primer. This one is "generic" and can be used with all C++ compilers including those for Unix machines.

The Waite Group's Master C++ (Waite Group Press, 1992). Teaches C++ step by step at your PC, quizzes you interactively, and makes sure you master each concept.

The Waite Group's Master C (Waite Group Press, 1990). Similar to previous, but for the original C language.

As you become more advanced, the following books are good reference guides:

The C Programming Language, Brian W. Kernighan and Dennis M. Ritchie (Prentice Hall, 1978 and 1988). This is about C, not C++, but it's considered the standard reference. The writing isn't too terrible, perhaps better than most. It's almost never referred to by its actual name, but instead by "Kernighan and Ritchie," or simply "K&R." It's a definite must for your bookshelf if you program regularly in either C or C++.

The C++ Programming Language, Bjarne Stroustrup, 2nd Ed. (Addison-Wesley, 1991). Stroustrup is the creator of C++, and like K&R, this is a good book to work through after you've been studying the language for at least a few months and want to make sure you really know your stuff. It's not exactly easy reading, but it's very complete.

Object-Oriented Programming in Microsoft C++ and *Object-Oriented Programming in Turbo C++* (Waite Group Press, 1992 and 1991 respectively). A masterful, hands-on introduction to the use of Borland or Microsoft programming tools. Some familiarity is useful, but both treat C++ as a stand-alone language.

There are also loads and loads of books on C++. It's pretty much pick and choose which ones are best for you. Many are specific for certain compilers, so don't buy one if it's for a compiler that you won't be using. Also, you may want to stay clear of the hardcover books, because they're probably very textbookish (not to mention expensive) and often *very* difficult to read.

Also, no matter who recommends a book, spend a good deal of time in the bookstore paging through the book and reading pieces of it, before you actually buy it. What's good for one person might be terrible for another.

INDEX

Page references having an asterisk (*)
after them point to program code.

Symbols

!=, 67
#, 224
%, 236
&, 113-114
&&, 70-72
(), 116
*, 113-114
++, 40
->, 117
//, 27
::, 98
;, 6, 14, 231
<, 67
<<, 23, 24, 174
<=, 67
=, 65
==, 65
>, 67
>=, 67
>>, 174
\0, 177
\n, 236
{}, 6
||, 70-72
~, 119

A

addresses, 109-110
AND operator (&&), 70-72
arithmetic operations
    denoting, 26-27
    floating-point, 59-60
    integer, 26-28, 58-59
    order of, 27-28
arrays
    basics of, 150-153
    integer, 153-155
    of objects, 155-156
    of pointers, 156-157
attributes
    defined, 7, 245
    denoting, 40
    pointers as, 193-194
    private, 181
    protected, 181
    public vs. private, 127-132

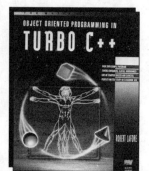

Please fill out this card if you wish to know of future updates to *Simple* C++, or to receive our catalog.

Company Name: _____

Division: _____ Mail Stop: _____

Last Name: _____ First Name: _____ Middle Initial: _____

Street Address: _____

City: _____ State: _____ Zip: _____

Daytime Telephone: (_____) _____

Date product was acquired: Month _____ Day _____ Year _____   Your Occupation: _____

Overall, how would you rate Simple C++?

☐ Excellent   ☐ Very Good   ☐ Good
☐ Fair   ☐ Below Average ☐ Poor

What did you like MOST about this product? _____
_____
_____

What did you like LEAST about this product? _____
_____
_____

How do you use this book (tutorial, reference, problem-solver...)? _____
_____
_____

How did you find the pace of this book? _____
_____

What version of C++ are you using? _____

DId you know C when you bought this book? _____

What computer languages are you familiar with?
_____
_____

What is your level of computer expertise?

☐ New   ☐ Dabbler   ☐ Hacker
☐ Power User   ☐ Programmer   ☐ Experienced
                              Professional

Where did you buy this book?

☐ Bookstore name: _____
☐ Discount store name: _____
☐ Computer store name: _____
☐ Catalog name: _____
☐ Direct from WGP   ☐ Other_____

What price did you pay for this book? _____

What influenced your purchase of this book?

☐ Recommendation   ☐ Mailing
☐ Advertisement   ☐ Book's format
☐ Magazine review   ☐ Reputation of
☐ Store Display   The Waite Group®
☐ Other:_____

How many computer books do you buy each year?
_____

How many other Waite Group books do you own?
_____

What is your favorite Waite Group book? _____
_____

Is there any program or subject you would like to see The Waite Group cover in a similar approach? _____
_____
_____

Any other comments? _____

Please send to: Waite Group Press
                   Attn: Simple C++
                   200 Tamal Plaza
                   Corte Madera, CA 94925

☐ Check here for a free Waite Group Press™ catalog

Simple C++